• Bartholomew

WALK
PERTHSHIRE

Produced in association
with Perthshire Tourist Board

PERTHSHIRE

'ALL OF SCOTLAND'

Bartholomew
An Imprint of HarperCollins*Publishers*

A Bartholomew Walk Guide

Published by Bartholomew
An Imprint of HarperCollins *Publishers*
77-85 Fulham Palace Road
Hammersmith
London W6 8JB
in association with
Perthshire Tourist Board,
Lower City Mills
West Mill Street
Perth PH1 5QP

First published 1986
Reprinted with amendments 1987, 1988
Revised editions 1991, 1993, 1996

Printed in Great Britain by The Edinburgh Press Limited

ISBN 0 7028 2944 7

HJ7960
86/4/65

Preface

A detailed account of 45 walks in Perth and Kinross District, each with accompanying map. The routes cater for all types of walkers and ramblers, from short strolls in and around the towns and villages to the more demanding forest and hill walks; some more strenuous ascents of the higher mountains are also included.

Helpful guidance is given on the difficulty of each route, equipment necessary, and the availability of parking, picnic sites and public transport. The descriptions also include uncomplicated background information to introduce you to the history, geology and ecology of the area, and you are directed towards local hotel and shopping facilities, and other places of interest, to assist you in making the most of your day out.

Acknowledgements

Perthshire Tourist Board acknowledges the considerable work undertaken by **Richard Hallewell**, who researched and wrote the original route descriptions in this book; **Rebecca Johnstone**, who prepared the original maps and illustrations; and the Countryside Rangers and Planning Officers of **Perth and Kinross District Council**, who have assisted with the updating of the original material.

Perthshire Tourist Board,
Lower City Mills,
West Mill Street,
Perth,
PH1 5QP.

Location of Walks

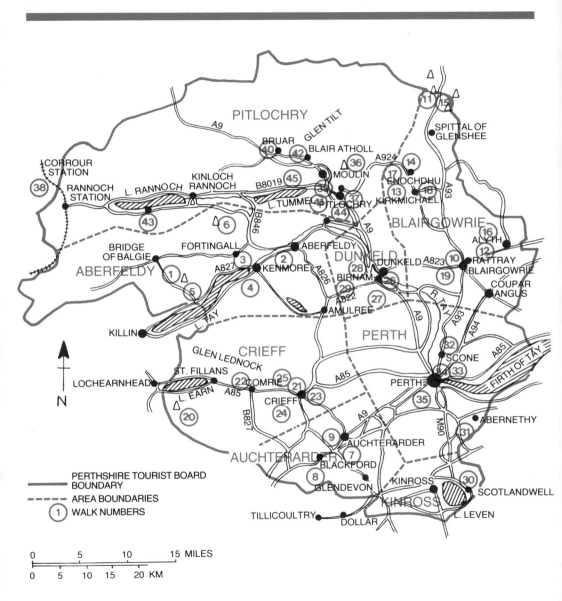

PERTHSHIRE TOURIST BOARD BOUNDARY

AREA BOUNDARIES

① WALK NUMBERS

| 0 | 5 | 10 | 15 MILES |
| 0 | 5 | 10 | 15 | 20 KM |

Contents

	Page
Preface	3
Acknowledgements	3
Location of Walks	4
Introduction	6
Perthshire	6
Grading, Equipment and Safety Precautions	8
Country Code	9
How the Walks are Presented	10
Areas of Perthshire	11
Gaelic - English	12
Key to Maps & Tourist Information Centres	13

INDEX OF WALKS

AREA ROUTE	GRADE	PAGE
Aberfeldy and Loch Tay		
1. Ben Lawers	C/A	14
2. Birks o' Aberfeldy	B	16
3. Drummond Hill	B/C	18
4. Kenmore to Amulree	B/C	20
5. Loch Tay to Bridge of Balgie	B/C	22
6. Schiehallion	A	24
Auchterarder		
7. Auchterarder to Glendevon	A	26
8. Blackford to Tillicoultry	A	28
9. Oak Walk, Auchterarder	C	30
Blairgowrie, Glenshee and Strathmore		
10. Banks of Ericht	C	32
11. Cairnwell	A	34
12. Den of Alyth	C	36
13. Enochdhu to Kirkmichael	B	38
14. Enochdhu to Spittal of Glenshee	A/B	40
15. Glas Maol and Creag Leacach	A	42
16. Hill of Alyth	B	44
17. Kindrogan Hill Trail	B	46
18. Kirkmichael to Lair	B	48
19. The Knockie	B	50
Crieff and Loch Earn		
20. Ben Vorlich	A	52
21. Crieff Nature Trail	C	54
22. Glen Lednock Circular Walk	B	56
23. The Knock	B	58
24. Lady Mary's Walk	C	60
25. Laggan Hill	C	62

AREA ROUTE	GRADE	PAGE
Dunkeld and Birnam		
26. Around Birnam	C	64
27. Birnam Hill	B	66
28. Dunkeld Heritage Trail	C	68
29. The Hermitage and River Braan	C	70
Kinross-shire		
30. Bishop Hill	B	72
Perth		
31. Abernethy Glen	B/C	74
32. Bonhard Circular Walk	B	76
33. Kinnoull Hill, Woodland Park (East)	C	78
34. Kinnoull Hill, Woodland Park (West)	B	80
35. Old Perth Trail	C	82
Pitlochry, Tummel and Rannoch		
36. Ben Vrackie	A	84
37. The Black Spout and Donavourd	C	86
38. Corrour to Rannoch Station	A	88
39. Craigower Hill	B	90
40. Falls of Bruar	C	92
41. Garry-Tummel Walks System	C	94
42. Glen Tilt	A/B	96
43. Rannoch Forest	B/C	98
44. Strathtay	B	100
45. Tummel Forest	B/C	102

Introduction

The appeal of walking is surely universal, whether it be a short stroll along town streets, or the well-laid paths of a grassed or wooded park, on longer, rougher tracks across high moors and mountain tops, or through some dense and silent forest. The importance of a walk is not in its length or difficulty, but in the opportunity it offers to see new sights and stretch old legs, to breathe the fresh air and contemplate the surrounding scenery.

The strength of Perthshire as a walking centre lies in the extraordinary variety of backgrounds it provides for the potential walker: largely rural (from the rocky and heath-covered slopes of the western hills to the low-lying farmland of Strathearn and Strathmore) but also with interesting routes through towns and villages to add further diversity.

The aim of this book is to direct the walker (of whatever ability or experience) towards the finest walks through these various landscapes, and to try and ensure that he or she finds a route suited to personal preferences and ability. The lengths and heights of each walk are noted, along with the facilities available at each, and the nature of the terrain covered. Please follow the guidelines outlined in the Grading System used throughout the book, and take note of the advice offered in this introduction (and by others who have walked the routes before you). You should then find the undertaking of your chosen route a most enjoyable and satisfying experience.

Perthshire

Perthshire is an inland district; stretching 60 miles (100km) from Beinn a' Chreachain (3540ft/1078m) on the edge of Rannoch Moor in the west, to Meigle in green Strathmore to the east; and some 45 miles (75km) from The Cairnwell (3059ft/ 932m) in the north, to the Cleish Hills, on the border between Fife and the old county of Kinross (included in the Perthshire area) to the south. The area it covers can be thought of as a wide bowl, tipped to one side: the catchment area of the River Tay.

The Tay, the longest river in Scotland, flows majestically some 120 miles from the slopes of Ben Lui, in Argyll, to Perth and then opens out into the Firth of Tay at Dundee on the North Sea. Wherever one walks in Perthsire, tributaries of the river are to be found: the Tummel, the Earn, the Garry, the Lyon and many more, bringing their waters from the mountains of Breadalbane and Atholl to the farmland around Perth. These constitute an economic, as well as an aesthetic resource, as many of the rivers which provide the headwaters of the Tay are dammed where they pass through the narrow Highland glens, and provide a source of hydro-electric power.

Perthshire is clearly divided into two parts, however, and it is the larger north-western section of the district which exhibits Highland characteristics. To the south and east the land is very different: flat and green, with low rolling hills. The two parts meet along a line which, through the years, has not only divided 'Highland' from 'Lowland' in a geographical sense but has also been a boundary between the separate cultures of the Gaelic-speaking 'Highlander' and English-speaking 'Lowlander'. This is the Highland Boundary Fault, better known as the 'Highland Line'.

The line stretches, roughly speaking, from Helensburgh on the Firth of Clyde to Stonehaven, just south of Aberdeen, through Crieff, Dunkeld, Blairgowrie, and Alyth in Perthshire. In geological terms it divides an area mainly composed of schists, with intrusions of granite and other materials (the Highlands), from one composed of limestone and particularly (in the case of Perthshire) old red sandstone, again with granitic intrusions forming steep-sided hills. Gradually, the sandstone belt sank below the level of schists, creating a rift valley across the centre of Scotland, reaching as far south as the Southern Uplands.

Then the glaciers of the ice-age began the process of etching the surface of the land into its present shape. Most of the high plateau was scraped away, although it is still possible to imagine what it was once like by looking north from The Cairnwell across the flat-topped hills of the north Grampians, towards the level heights of the Cairngorms. What was left elsewhere was a landscape of stark, rugged hills - taller where the rock, being harder, could provide greater resistance to the ice - intersected by wide, flat-bottomed valleys, along which the principal glaciers had run: many of them emanating from Rannoch Moor, a vast reservoir of ice in the west of Perthshire.

These steep-sided valleys, which run practically in a straight line, and dwarf the rivers which meander along their silted floors, are typical elements of a glacial landscape. Look also for the wide selection of rock types to be found embedded in the soil, or by the sides of lochs and rivers: these have been carried great distances by the ice, before being mixed and deposited as the ice melted.

Having reached its present shape, Perthshire became covered - along with the rest of Britain - in thick forests: oaks, birches and other deciduous trees along the valley floors, and Scots Pine - the only native conifer - on the upper slopes. Remnants of these forests are still visible along the routes mentioned in this book (oakwoods around Glen Lednock, Killiecrankie and the Den of Alyth in particular, and the Old Caledonian Pine Forest in the Black Wood of Rannoch), but most of the original tree cover has been removed by generations of farmers and foresters. However, in more recent times the Forestry Commission and various private landowners have taken to planting extensive forests of imported species of conifers - such as the Norway Spruce, Sitka Spruce, Larch and Lodgepole Pine - as well as replanting the native pine. Sad to say, not all of these forests are places of exquisite beauty, but landscaping techniques are gradually improving, and walks are included in this book through some of the more interesting plantations.

Where the 'bare' hillside remains, the cover is largely of heather, mosses and lichens, with local patches of bell heather, crowberry, bearberry, and blaeberry etc. The exception to this general rule, however, is Ben Lawers and the surrounding hills, where the soil is rich enough in lime to support large areas of mat grassland.

North of the Highland Line, arable farming is only possible in the alluvial deposits left along the valley floors, and the greater part of the land - being too steep, and too poor in its soil cover to allow cultivation - is given over to grazing, particularly of sheep, and to moorland on which red grouse and red deer are maintained for sporting purposes. In the lowland areas, however, the majority of the land is cultivated for the production of cereals and root crops, with fruit also being grown, particularly in Strathmore.

The geographical shape of Perthshire - straddling the Highland Line, and with major routeways through Strathearn and Strathmore, and northwards along Strathtay and Glen Garry - has in turn helped to shape its history.

The observant walker will, therefore, note the standing stones erected for unknown reasons by early settlers, and the hilltop forts held by the native Picts in defence against the Romans, whose road and garrisons lay below in Strathearn. Defences were later erected against the Vikings, and then the English, with Scone and Dunkeld playing vital roles in Scottish political and ecclesiastical history. The conflicts between neighbouring clans, and their rebellions against the crown, were brought to an end in the 18th century, when General Wade constructed his roads into the Highlands.

Thereafter, trade and industry flourished, bringing prosperity to towns and villages in the area, whilst many rural settlements were abandoned, particularly in the more isolated glens.

Thus, natural and human history have together created a fascinating, often beautiful, and extremely varied landscape, providing the setting for the walks in this book.

Grading, Equipment and Safety Precautions

Each walk in the book is graded according to the following system:

A - These walks should only be undertaken by those with previous experience of hill walking. Strong hiking boots should be worn, and warm clothing and waterproofs should be taken along, in case of sudden changes in the weather. Also carry the relevant Ordnance Survey map and a compass, being sure you are familiar with the use of both.

B - Less strenuous and demanding than Grade A, and can be undertaken by anyone who is used to regular exercise. Take strong boots, waterproof clothing and the relevant Ordnance Survey map on the longer moorland walks, although strong, comfortable footwear is the only necessity on the shorter walks.

C - These walks can be undertaken by anyone - inexperienced walkers and families included - and require no further direction than the maps included in the book. Be sure to wear comfortable clothing, and use waterproof footwear if the route is not confined to built-up areas.

These grades can only give a general indication of the difficulty of a route; many family groups will be quite capable of completing walks outside group C for instance, while a grade B walk can easily become grade A if the weather conditions are bad.

Always check the weather forecast, therefore, before setting off on the longer hikes (there are regular forecasts on TV and radio, and telephone forecasts offer a more detailed analysis) and prepare yourself for the walk accordingly. Do remember that an excess of sunshine - causing sunburn or dehydration - can be just as debilitating as a snow or rain shower, so carry adequate cover for your body in all conditions when on the hills.

Snow cover on the higher slopes often remains well into the summer, and should be avoided by inexperienced walkers, as it often covers hidden watercourses and other pitfalls which are likely to cause injury; also - especially when soft - it is extremely gruelling to cross, and can sap the energy very quickly. Walking on snow-covered hills should not be attempted without an ice-axe and crampons.

The other weather-associated danger on the hills is the mist, which can appear very swiftly and cut visibility to a few yards. In such conditions, it is essential to have a map and compass for navigation.

Obviously these problems are unlikely to arise on the shorter, simpler routes, but it is always wise when out walking to anticipate the worst and to be prepared for it. You may never need the extra equipment, but it is worth taking it with you anyway, just in case. Spare food, a first-aid kit, a whistle, and a torch with a spare battery, should be carried on all hill walks. In addition, details of your route and expected time of completion should be left with someone who you should advise on your safe return.

There is one final danger for hill walkers which is entirely predictable. From August onwards there is grouse-shooting and deer-stalking on the moors. If you are undertaking one of these hill routes, then check with the local estate or estate workers before doing so, thereby avoiding a nuisance for the sportsmen, and possible danger for yourself.

Country Code

All walkers, when leaving public roads to pass through farmland, forestry or moorland, should respect the interests of those whose livelihood depends on the land. Carelessness can easily cause damage. We therefore urge you to follow the Country Code:

Guard against all risk of fire.

Keep all dogs under proper control (especially during lambing season April-May).

Leave all gates as you find them.

Keep to the paths across farmland.

Avoid damaging fences, hedges and walls.

Leave no litter.

Safeguard water supplies.

Protect wildlife, wild plants and trees.

Go carefully on country roads.

Respect the life of the countryside.

How the Walks are Presented

Each walk description is preceded by a list of factual details, including the following:

Maps

All map references are from the Ordnance Survey Landranger Series, 1:50,000. When two sheet numbers are given, it means either that there are two possible maps for a route (eg 53 **or** 58) or that two maps are required to cover the walk (eg 53 **and** 58).

Length

Usually the distance shown is for a round trip, but if it is for one direction only, transport must be found from the far end of the walk, or else the mileage must be doubled to include the return trip.

'Height Climbed'

This refers (in non-circular walks) to the direction described in the text. If walked in the other direction these figures may need revising. **Metric equivalents:**

1 foot = 0.3m
1 mile = 1.6km

Grade - See explanation above.
When estimating times for routes, allow 25 minutes per mile, with an additional 30 minutes for every 1000ft/300m of ascent. These timings will vary according to fitness, and do not take account of prolonged stops for rest or eating.

Public Transport

Many of the walks are located close to the main towns, which are all connected by bus and/or train services, so that no car is required for these. Information is given on the availability of public transport where walks are situated at some distance from the main towns, or where the route is not circular. Full details of bus and train services are available at Tourist Information Centres.

Picnic Sites

Only formal picnic sites, ie those with seating and tables, are given. All the walks pass by attractive spots which are suitable for picnics, but be sure not to leave litter behind.

Other Literature

Many of the low-level walks are maintained by particular organisations, such as the Forestry Commission, National Trust for Scotland, or Perthshire and Kinross Council and where they have produced information leaflets this is stated. These leaflets provide further information particularly on vegetation and wildlife, and are generally available at Information Centres.

It has not been possible in this book to cover the more difficult hill climbs and cross-country routes, of which there are many in Perthshire, providing challenges for the more experienced and energetic hill walkers. These are dealt with in numerous other publications, readily available in bookshops in Perthshire, of which the most authoritative are the Scottish Mountaineering Club District Guides.

However, a list of some of the recognised cross-country routes is given on page 104, to indicate the choice available.

Areas of Perthshire

In between walks, make the most of the many varied attractions that Perthshire has to offer. The routes are grouped according to eight areas, each with its own distinctive characteristics and places of interest. These are shown on the map on page 4, and a brief introductory sketch of each main town and its surroundings is given below. Further details on each area may be obtained by calling at, or telephoning, the relevant Tourist Information Centre as listed on page 13.

Aberfeldy is in the heart of Highland Perthshire. The Birks o' Aberfeldy waterfalls and woodland nature trail, Wade's Bridge over the Tay, and the indoor swimming pool and recreation centre are only a short walk from the town centre. Kenmore provides boating facilities on Loch Tay, with lofty Ben Lawers, graceful Schiehallion and secluded Glen Lyon to the north.

Auchterarder, known as the 'Lang Toon', provides a peaceful place for shopping, particularly for antiques. On the edge of fertile Strathearn, with the Ochil Hills to the south, it is an excellent centre for golfing, fishing and touring holidays in particular. The town has a fascinating Heritage Centre, with the famous Gleneagles Hotel close by.

Blairgowrie lies beside the River Ericht, whose banks provide an attractive woodland walk. Its modern recreational centre, regular Highland Nights, and many summer events in the locality, make the town an ideal holiday centre. Coupar Angus, Alyth and Meigle are attractive smaller centres in fertile Strathmore, famous for its soft fruit. Strathardle and Glenshee stretch up into the hills to the north, where extensive skiing facilities are situated beside the A93.

Crieff stands where the magnificent Highlands meet the green pastures of Strathearn, providing fine contrasts of scenery. With a pottery, glass works and distillery welcoming visitors, and many recreational facilities, there is something for everyone. To the west is Comrie and scenic Loch Earn, with many walks in the hills around. Historic Wade's Road leads north through delightful Sma'Glen.

Dunkeld and Birnam, linked by Telford's magnificent bridge across the Tay, provide a relaxing haven at the rugged edge of the Highlands. Dunkeld Cathedral, the restored Little Houses, and the Birnam Oak are notable points of interest, and delightful woodland and riverside walks lead to the Hermitage and the wildlife reserve at Loch of the Lowes.

Kinross has an impressive setting surrounded by hills, which provide superb views. The area has a wealth of historical buildings, notably Loch Leven Castle, where Mary Queen of Scots was imprisoned. Vane Farm Nature Centre and Crook of Devon Fish Farm are other local attractions, and there is a wide variety of towns, villages and countryside within easy reach.

Perth is a focus of both road and rail communications, and its scenic situation beside the Tay overlooked by wooded Kinnoull Hill rivals that of any town in Britain. Leisure facilities include the unique Perth Leisure Pool, the Perth Theatre, two museums, art galleries, and an extensive range of shops and eating places. There are numerous historic buildings and fine gardens in and around the town, with Scone Palace combining both.

Pitlochry is set amidst hills, glens, lochs, rivers and tumbling streams, with numerous historic and scenic points of interest from the Pass of Killiecrankie to the Hydro-electric dam. There is evening entertainment at the famous Festival Theatre and Highland Nights. Blair Atholl to the north boasts magnificent Blair Castle, a working Meal Mill and a Folk Museum, whilst the Road to the Isles extends westwards by Loch Tummel and Loch Rannoch.

GAELIC-ENGLISH

The names of settlements and features of the landscape in Perthshire are generally pure Gaelic or of Gaelic derivation. The list below includes many of the more common words, some with anglicised versions, which will help you to interpret the meaning of these place-names.

Aber, Obair - *Confluence*
Abhainn - *River*
Achadh, Ach, Auch - *Field*
Allt - *Stream*
Ard - *High*
Bad - *Thicket*
Bal, Ball - *Town*
Ban - *White, pale*
Beag, Beg - *Small*
Bealach - *Pass, gap*
Beinn, Ben - *Mountain*
Beith - *Birch*
Blair - *Level field*
Braigh - *Summit*
Breac - *Speckled*
Buidhe - *Yellow, golden*
Cam - *Bent*
Caoruinn - *Rowan*
Carn, Cairn - *Hill, heap of stones*
Carse - *Level plain*
Ceann, Kin - *Head*
Clach - *Stone*
Cladh - *Burial Place*
Cnoc, Knock - *Hillock*
Coille - *Wood*
Coire, Corrie - *Kettle, hollow*
Craggan - *Little rock*
Creag, Craig - *Rock, cliff*
Croit, Croft - *Highland smallholding*
Cruaidh, Croy - *Hard*

Dal, Dail - *Meadow*
Darach - *Oak*
Dearg - *Red*
Donn - *Brown*
Doire - *Grove*
Druim, Drum - *Ridge*
Dubh - *Black*
Dun - *Fort, steep hill*
Eas, Ess - *Waterfall*
Eilean - *Island*
Elrig - *Deer trap*
Fearna - *Alder*
Feith - *Vein, bog*
Fionn - *White, fair*
Fuaran - *Spring*
Gaoth - *Wind*
Garbh - *Rough*
Garth, Garadh, Garry - *Enclosure*
Geal - *White, bright*
Glas - *Grey/green*
Gleann, Glen - *Valley*
Gobhar, Gabhar - *Goat*
Inver - *Confluence, river mouth*
Kil, Cill - *Church*
Lagan, Laggan - *Hollow*
Lairig - *Hill pass*
Leacann, Lechkin - *Slope*
Leathad, Led - *Slope, declivity*
Leathann - *Broad*
Leck - *Flag*

Leitir, Letter - *Extensive slope*
Liath - *Grey*
Lochan - *Small lake*
Lurg - *Strip of land*
Mam - *Large round hill*
Meadhonach - *Middle*
Meall - *Lump, shapeless hill*
Moine - *Moss, peat*
Monadh - *Extensive hill, moorland*
Mor - *Large*
Obair, Aber - *Confluence*
Odhar, Our - *Dun, drab*
Raineach, Rannoch - *Fern*
Reamhar - *Fat*
Ruadh - *Red*
Sgurr - *Peak, sharp top*
Sneachd - *Snow*
Srath, Strath - *Wide valley*
Sron, Strone - *Nose, point*
Stob - *Point, peak*
Stuc - *Pinnacle*
Tarmachan - *Ptarmigan*
Tigh, Ty - *House*
Tir - *Land*
Tomb, Tom - *Hillock*
Tulach, Tullich - *Knoll*
Uaine - *Green*
Uamh - *Cave*
Uisge, Esk - *Water*

Key to Maps

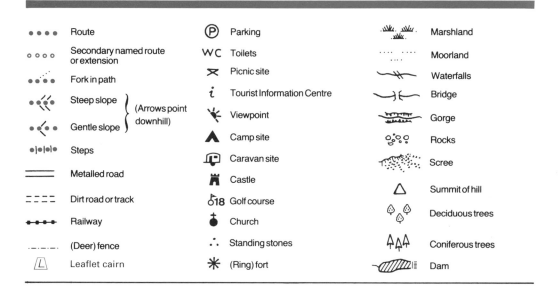

••••	Route	℗	Parking	Marshland
○○○○	Secondary named route or extension	WC	Toilets	Moorland
	Fork in path	✕	Picnic site	Waterfalls
	Steep slope	𝑖	Tourist Information Centre	Bridge
	(Arrows point downhill)		Viewpoint	Gorge
	Gentle slope	▲	Camp site	Rocks
•│•│•│•	Steps		Caravan site	Scree
	Metalled road		Castle	△ Summit of hill
─ ─ ─ ─	Dirt road or track	♂18	Golf course	Deciduous trees
♦━♦━♦	Railway		Church	Coniferous trees
	(Deer) fence	∴	Standing stones	Dam
⌐L̸	Leaflet cairn	✳	(Ring) fort	

TOURIST INFORMATION CENTRES

𝑖 The Centres listed below have a wide range of information and publications to help you enjoy your stay in Perthshire, and can also arrange your accommodation.

The Information staff will be able to give you further advice on the routes listed in this book, and supply you with Ordnance Survey maps and detailed leaflets where applicable. In addition, they will be pleased to suggest other walks in the locality.

Whilst the details in this book were believed to be correct at the time of going to press, alterations may occur from time to time as a result of changes, for example, to paths, fences, land-use patterns, or rights of access. The Local Tourist Information Centres should be able to advise you of any such changes, and we would be grateful if you would tell them if you encounter any difficulties whilst out walking.

ABERFELDY, The Square,
Tel: (01887)820276. Open all year.
AUCHTERARDER, 90 High Street,
Tel: (01764)663450. Open all year.
BLAIRGOWRIE, 26 Wellmeadow,
Tel: (01250)872960/873701. Open all year.
CRIEFF, Town Hall, High Street,
Tel: (01764)652578. Open all year.
DUNKELD, The Cross.
Tel:(01350)727688. Open Easter-Xmas.
KINROSS, Service Area, Junction 6, M90.
Tel: (01577)863680. Open all year.
PERTH, 45 High Street,
Tel: (01738)638353. Open all year.
Caithness Glass Visitor Centre.
Tel: (01738) 638481. Open all year.
PITLOCHRY, 22 Atholl Road.
Tel: (01796)472215/472751. Open all year.

1 *Ben Lawers* – *Nature Trail and Summit Walk*

Grid Ref: 609 377 (car park and Information Centre) **Map Sheet:** 51

A short nature trail set in high mountain scenery, with a longer alternative walk to the summit of Ben Lawers.

Length: Nature Trail 1 mile; Summit Walk 7 miles (there and back)
Height Climbed: 2580ft/787m (summit walk)
Grade: Nature Trail C; Summit Walk A
Public Transport: None
Parking: At foot of walk (parking fee)
Toilet Facilities: In car park
Information Leaflet available from the Visitor Centre

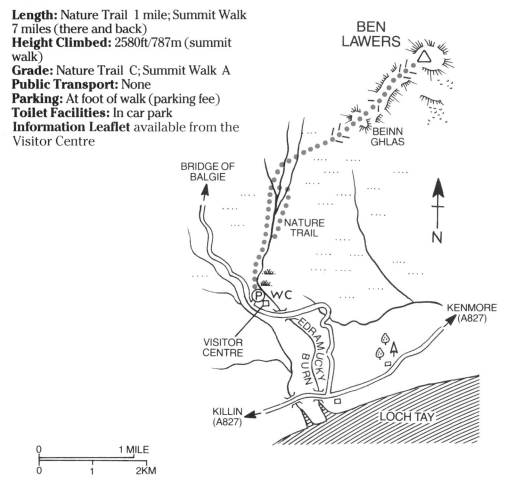

Ben Lawers is not only the highest mountain in Perthshire (3987ft), it is also one of the most fascinating. Untouched by the glaciers of the last ice-age, and with a unique soil type (a very soft, lime-rich schist), the mountain retains perhaps the finest selection of alpine flowers to be found in Britain. The mountain's ecological importance persuaded the National Trust for Scotland to purchase it, and they now operate an information centre at the foot of the walks.

To reach the centre, take the A827 road along the north side of Loch Tay between Kenmore and Killin, and turn up the small road to Bridge of Balgie (about four miles from Killin and 10 miles from Kenmore). The centre is two miles along this road on your right hand side, and books and booklets on the mountain and its flora are available as well as audio-visual programmes.

The nature trail is a short tour of the area around the centre, and an accompanying booklet gives a commentary on the ecological features along the route. The path is relatively easy under foot, but even on this short trail you must expect the going to be wet in places.

The path to the summit is a much tougher proposition than its length might suggest, since it rises around 2700ft in 3½ miles, and crosses some difficult terrain. This route should not be attempted without correct footwear and some previous experience of hill-walking. However, it is a truly rewarding climb for those who attempt it.

The path crosses some level moor before rising steeply to the summit of Beinn Ghlas, dipping once more, and crossing a thin ridge between two steep corries, and then rising steeply again to the summit of Ben Lawers itself. The walk will take you considerably longer than you anticipate, and you should return by the same route, but it is no hardship to spend time in such splendid scenery.

On the walk watch out for the distinctive flowers of the region (but please don't pick them), and also for the buzzards, kestrels, red grouse and golden plovers, amongst others, which inhabit these higher levels. Once at the summit, be prepared for one of the finest views in Scotland; including every major hill in Perthshire (all of which are marked on an indicator), and reaching - on a clear day - from the North Sea to the Atlantic.

One final word: since this area is of such unique botanical importance (it is a National Nature Reserve) you are asked to stay to the paths indicated as closely as possible, and not to extend the erosion which is already visible in places.

Golden Plover

2 Birks of Aberfeldy

Grid Ref: 855 486 (start of upper walk) **Map Sheet:** 52

A steep walk along the gorge of the Moness Burn, passing through pleasant woodland and giving fine views of the Moness Falls.

Length: 2½ miles
Height Climbed: 550ft/167m
Grade: B
Public Transport: Regular bus routes from Dunkeld and Pitlochry
Parking: In Aberfeldy, and at foot of upper walk beside A826
Picnic Sites: By car park for upper walk
Toilet Facilities: In Aberfeldy
Information Leaflet on Nature Trail available from Upper Birks car park leaflet cairn.

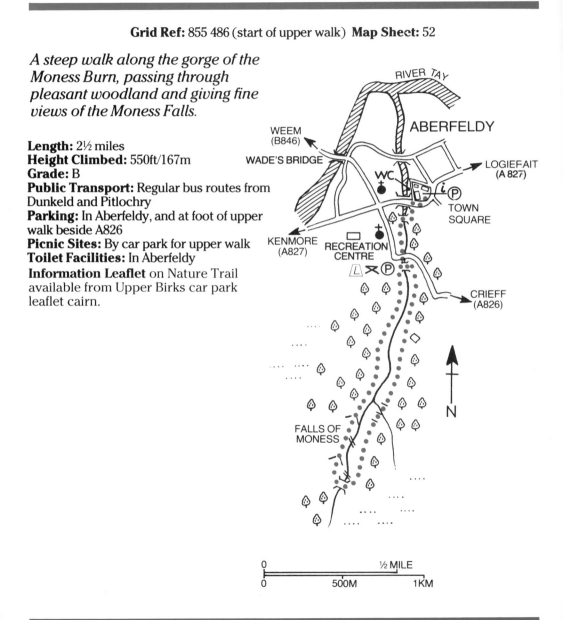

The Falls of Moness are among the most spectacular and accessible waterfalls in Perthshire, and the pleasure of visiting them is considerably heightened by the beauty of the steeply sided, wooded glen which holds them.

The walk is divided into two sections. The first - a short path through the lower woods - starts just off the Aberfeldy Square, on the road to Kenmore. Follow the sign and turn left just before the bridge over the Moness Burn. This path crosses the burn and travels a few hundred yards until it reaches the A826 road to Crieff. Cross this road with care and bear left to the car park and entrance to The Birks.

A short way along the path it divides into a scenic route and a nature trail, but if you are simply out for a walk this need not bother you, since the two routes join above the top fall. The path is quite steep and sometimes muddy in places, and passes close to the cliff edges, but it is well maintained and solid steps and fences are provided where necessary. Strong footwear is certainly advised.

All along the route there is lush vegetation with woods comprised mainly of oak, beech and the 'birks' (or birch trees) of the walk's title. The name comes from a poem composed by Robert Burns:

'The hoary cliffs are crowned wi' flowers,
White o'er the linns the burnie pours,
And rising, weets wi' misty showers,
The birks of Aberfeldy'

and the spot where he composed it, a rocky ledge set into the rock face, is by the path on the east side of the glen.

As the poem suggests, the main attraction of the walk is its waterfalls, and the finest of these is the highest, which is spanned by a footbridge. This position affords excellent views of the water's sheer drop into a steeply sided rocky bowl.

The mixed woodland provides a rich habitat for birdlife, and indeed the area is designated as a site of special scientific interest, so that it is particularly important to keep to the paths.

Sheltered as it is, the glen can be a rewarding place to visit even in poor weather, when heavy rainfall makes the falls especially impressive. However, the scene is at its best on a fine day in spring or autumn, when the sunlight filters through the trees, illuminating the leaves.

Whatever the weather, the walk may easily be combined with a visit to Wade's Bridge, shopping in Aberfeldy, and perhaps lunch or afternoon tea at one of the town's many excellent hotels and cafés.

A Recreation Centre with an indoor swimming pool and facilities for many sports is situated off the Crieff Road, close to this walk.

The staff at the Tourist Information Centre in the Square can give advice on other popular walks in and around the town.

3 *Drummond Hill*

Grid Ref: 771 460 (start of walk, Kenmore) **Map Sheet:** 51 or 52

A system of pathways through a Forestry Commission conifer plantation, along good tracks, with fine views of Loch Tay, the Tay valley and the surrounding hills.

Length: 2 – 10 miles
Height Climbed: 950ft/300m (to highest point on routes)
Grade: B/C
Public Transport: Postbus service from Aberfeldy
Parking: At start of walk (Kenmore and picnic site)
Picnic Facilities: At viewpoint and at picnic site
Toilet Facilities: Kenmore and picnic site

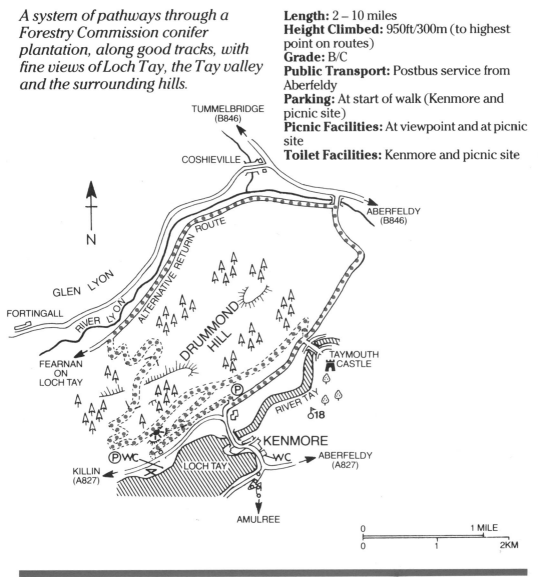

Drummond Hill is a long, low, hill, rising between Fortingall and lower Glen Lyon to the north, and Loch Tay, Kenmore and the Tay valley to the south. The hill - which reaches a height of 1485ft/458m - has been planted and landscaped by the Forestry Commission with a variety of trees, predominantly conifers. A number of paths are open to the public, and the position of the hill, at the confluence of the Lyon and the Tay, ensures that there are fine views to be had down both valleys.

There are three points of access to the pathways, and the Forestry Commission have divided them into three separate signposted routes. The shortest starts from either the picnic site on Loch Tay or from the entrance at Kenmore, and leads to the viewpoint, dramatically situated on a rocky outcrop overlooking Loch Tay and the village of Kenmore at its eastern end. Kenmore was rebuilt in 1760 by the 3rd Earl of Breadalbane, and it remains one of the neatest planned villages in Perthshire. Each June it is the starting point for a spectacular raft race attracting thousands of spectators, whilst in January a ceremony is held to mark the start of the salmon fishing season. The village boasts the oldest inn in Scotland, founded in 1572.

A second route starts from the same places, but leads eastwards instead, to a point overlooking Taymouth Castle. The castle, built for the Earl of Breadalbane in 1801, is now sadly empty, but this great blue-grey Gothic extravagance remains one of the architectural high-spots in Perthshire. Queen Victoria was entertained here in 1842, and described her reception (with typical 19th century whimsy) as being like a great chieftain in olden feudal times receiving his sovereign. 'It was princely and romantic'. There is now an attractive golf course in the grounds.

The longest walk leads past the viewpoint over the ridge of the hill, and down into Glen Lyon. The village of Fortingall, on the far side of the glen, is architecturally interesting. It was built in its present form by Sir Donald Currie, at the end of the 19th century, and was designed in the style of the village of Selworthy, in Devon. Other points of interest are the yew tree in the church yard, which, at over 3000 years old, is the oldest living thing in Europe; and a persistent legend that Pontius Pilate was born in the area. Here, too, is an old hotel with a fine reputation.

From the Glen Lyon end of the walk, you can either return by the same path or take a longer route home: turn right at the end of the path and it is about five miles, along minor roads, around the east end of Drummond Hill and back to the car park.

Taymouth Castle

4 *Kenmore to Amulree*

Grid Ref: 775 452 (Kenmore end)/900 366 (Amulree) **Map Sheet:** 52

A quiet metalled road across a high pass, with a path alongside Loch Freuchie, affording excellent views of the surrounding hills.

Length: 10 miles
Height Climbed: 1400ft/426m
Grade: B/C
Public Transport: Both Kenmore and Amulree are on postbus routes.
Toilet Facilities: In Kenmore

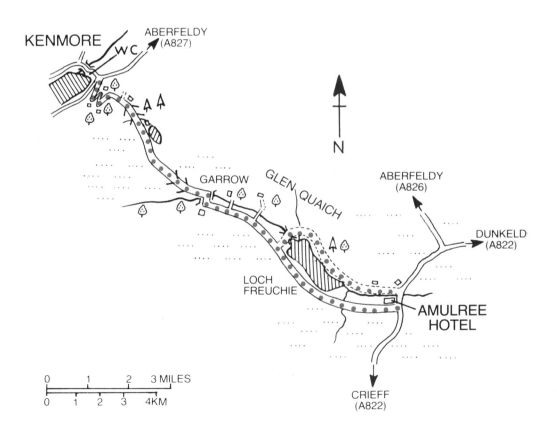

Although this route is a metalled road for the most part, it is quiet enough to be treated as a walk, and if you only wish a short walk, it is possible to drive to a stretch of this most dramatic route which appeals to you, park the car and go for a stroll. Be warned however, if you are uncertain of driving on single track roads: this road - which rises to 1750ft at its highest point - is very narrow and very steep, and contains some unnerving hairpin bends, so drive carefully and don't block the road when you park. Watch also for the gates across the road and be sure to close them behind you.

The northern end of the walk starts just outside Kenmore on the A827 road to Aberfeldy. There is a sharp bend and a small road heading along the south side of Loch Tay breaks away from the main road. Turn onto this road, and, just as it begins, a third road branches off uphill - this is the one to follow.

The route zig-zags past some houses and through a small wood before continuing to rise steadily across open moorland, finally reaching its highest point after some three miles.

From here you have marvellous views to the north of the hills around Glen Lyon and the Tay and Tummel valleys, and to the south across Glen Quaich to the last of the Grampians which mark the Highland Line. At this height the hills appear bare of all but heather, but as the road continues, and you drop steeply into Glen Quaich, the valley bottom becomes gradually more cultivated.

About two miles beyond the bridge at Garrow, the route divides. A footpath of some three miles recrosses the river and passes down the north-east side of Loch Freuchie, while the road continues down the south-west side.

The two paths ultimately arrive at opposite ends of the small hamlet of Amulree; once an important staging point for Highland cattle drovers on their way to the Crieff market, and then on the military road from Aberfeldy to Crieff which was built in the 18th century by General Wade. The route of that road is still largely followed by the A822 before you, but if the walk has given you a thirst or an appetite, you may wish to avail yourself of the services of the Amulree Hotel before travelling further. If you have taken the path beside Loch Freuchie, the road offers an alternative return route. Indeed, Amulree may be used as the starting-point for a circular walk of some 7½ miles around the Loch.

5 Loch Tay to Bridge of Balgie

Grid Ref: 576 467 (Bridge of Balgie); 621 364 (Loch Tay end of walk) **Map Sheet:** 51

A long walk on a metalled surface, across the pass between Ben Lawers and the Tarmachan Hills, giving fine views of Loch Tay, Glen Lyon and the surrounding hills.

Length: 10 miles (one way)
Height Climbed: (from Loch Tay) 1100ft/ 370m
Grade: B/C
Public Transport: Postbus service to each end of the walk from Aberfeldy.
Parking: National Trust Visitor Centre (on route) parking free
Toilet Facilities: National Trust Visitor Centre; Innerwick.

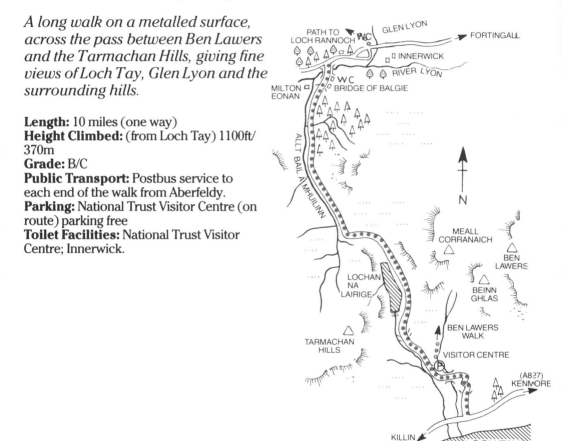

Although along a metalled road, this walk is not busy, and it passes through some truly dramatic scenery, under the shadow of Ben Lawers (3984ft/1214m), Perthshire's highest mountain.

One end of the route is on the north side of Loch Tay, about 10 miles from Kenmore on the A827. If you wish to park your car there is a car park nearby, two miles up the road (and also the walk) which leads uphill away from Loch Tayside, signposted to Bridge of Balgie. As you climb this road you will receive increasingly fine views of Loch Tay, which - at 15 miles long and 508ft/155m deep - is one of the largest in Scotland.

Beyond the car park the road continues to climb till it reaches the Hydro-electric reservoir of Lochan na Lairige. Here the road passes through a steeply-sided pass, with the slopes of Beinn Ghlas (a peak of Ben Lawers) to the right, and those of the Tarmachan Hills, beyond the loch to the left. A short way beyond the loch the highest part of the route is reached (1800ft/550m), and subsequently it continues down hill, by the side of Allt Bail a'Mhuilinn, into Glen Lyon.

Glen Lyon (more descriptively known in Gaelic as 'Chromghlearn nan clach': the Crooked Glen of the Stones) is 32 miles long, making it the longest glen in Scotland. It is also a place of great natural beauty, and considerable historic interest.

The Romans are believed to have had a camp at Fortingall, where it is said Pontius Pilate was born. Eonan, better known as Adamnan, biographer of St Columba, brought Christianity here from Iona in the 7th century (Milton Eonan, where he lived, is to the left of the road as it nears Bridge of Balgie). In the 16th century the glen was the property of the Campbells, who feuded with the landless MacGregors. Captain Robert Campbell of Glen Lyon was the perpetrator of the Glencoe massacre in 1692. As with most Highland glens the people were gradually moved out to make way for sheep in the century following the defeat of the Jacobites in 1746.

Bridge of Balgie is about 15 miles from Coshieville, where the Glen Lyon road joins the B846 from Aberfeldy to Tummel Bridge.

Apart from the scenery, this route is also of particular interest to naturalists, and at the car park above Loch Tay there is a visitor's centre giving information on the natural history of the area, and particularly on its alpine flora (see Route No 1). Watch also for red deer, buzzards, kestrels and red grouse on the moorland.

One final word of warning: this route is along a single track road, which can be a little strange for someone unused to such driving conditions. Those taking a car with them are therefore asked to be careful, particularly of the sheep which wander freely across the road.

6 *Schiehallion*

Grid Ref: 752 558 (car park) **Map Sheet:** 51 or 52

A climb up one of Scotland's most beautiful mountains, along rough paths, with marvellous summit views.

Length: 6 miles (there and back)
Height Climbed: 2465ft/754m
Grade: A
Public Transport: None
Parking: Car park at start of walk
Toilet Facilities: At car park

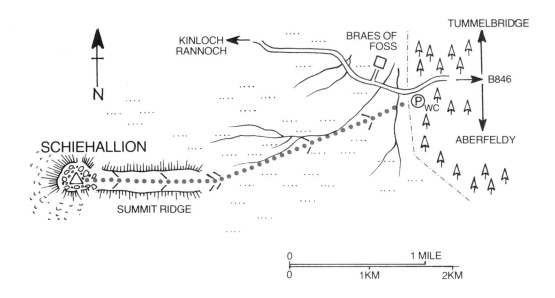

Schiehallion is one of the finest and best known of Scottish mountains, not because of its height (3554ft/1083m), but because of its distinctive conical shape. The hill, which stands on its own, can be seen well from the Queen's View on Loch Tummel, but is at its best when viewed from the road along the north side of Loch Rannoch.

It is Schiehallion's conical shape which led to its major claim to fame, since it made it ideal for use in early experiments to judge the weight of the Earth, which started in 1774. The experiments were not an unqualified success, but during the expedition, one of its members, Charles Hutton, invented Contour Lines as an aid to surveying the mountain. There is a cairn to commemorate this event at the entrance to the car park.

In earlier times Schiehallion was a place of worship for the Picts who inhabited all of eastern Scotland in the pre-Christian era; hence the name 'Schiehallion', which means 'The Fairy Mountain of the Caledonians'.

The walk itself appears deceptively easy from the starting point, but nobody should attempt it without heavy footwear and waterproof clothing, and previous hillwalking experience.

To reach the walk from Pitlochry, drive three miles north along the A9, and turn left across the Garry Bridge onto the B8019 for Tummel Bridge. Turn left at Tummel Bridge and follow the B846 for 4½ miles until you see a small road to your right leading to Kinloch Rannoch. From Aberfeldy, follow the B846 road for Tummel Bridge and you will find the road end five miles beyond Coshieville. Two miles along this road you will see a cairn on your left, and a road leading to a car park in a stand of trees.

The start of the path is clearly marked, but once on the moors it becomes less obvious. There are a number of paths crossing this stretch, but always aim towards the main ridge of the mountain, where the path which leads to the summit is well defined.

You should encounter no great problems until you approach the summit itself, which is a jumble of huge quartzite boulders, and can be difficult going, but there are a series of cairns along this section which clearly mark the best route.

The views from the peak are truly spectacular on a clear day: east to Ben Vrackie behind Pitlochry; north to Ben Alder, Beinn a' Ghlo and the Cairngorms and west across Rannoch Moor to the mountains above Glencoe. On the walk you can expect to see buzzards, larks amongst the heather and a considerable number of ptarmigan, a game bird which is found only above 2000ft.

While on Schiehallion, keep an eye open for patches of snow which are treacherous to walk on, and low cloud which can cut visibility to a minimum very swiftly as well as being particularly cold and damp.

Return by the same route.

7 *Auchterarder to Glen Devon* (and Dollar)

Grid Ref: 949 131 (end of Abbey Rd, Auchterarder) **Map Sheet:** 58

A lengthy walk over the Ochil Hills, giving fine views of Strathearn and across the Devon valley towards the Cleish Hills.

Length: 8 miles (one way)
Height Climbed: 1200ft/350m
Grade: A
Public Transport: Regular bus and train services to and from Auchterarder (Gleneagles Station). Dollar and Auchterarder linked by bus via Stirling.
Parking: Auchterarder, Glen Devon and Dollar. No parking at Coulshill Farm.
Toilet Facilities: Auchterarder

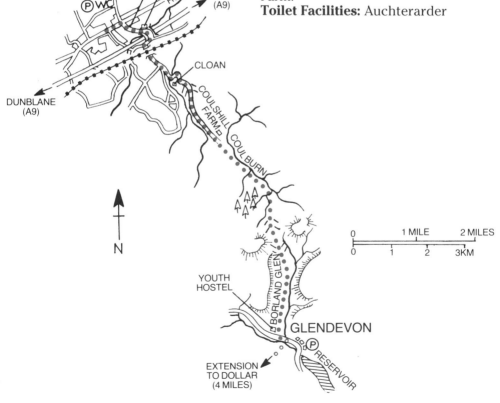

The Ochils are a long range of steeply-sided, round-topped hills, stretching thirty miles from the banks of the Firth of Tay in the north-east, to Stirling in the south-west. In common with other hills in Central Scotland, the Ochils are of volcanic rock and they date from the old red sandstone period. They were once linked with Moncreiffe Hill and the Sidlaws, now divided by the Rivers Earn and Tay. This popular walk crosses the range, from Auchterarder, on the edge of Strathearn, to Glendevon, meeting the A823 road which cuts through the range from Gleneagles to Yetts o' Muckhart. There is also a possible extension of the route to Dollar, from Glendevon Village.

Starting from Auchterader (see walk no.9), walk to the north end of the town and turn right, down Abbey Road. At the foot of this road there is a former textile mill. Cross the Ruthven Water here, and continue across the bridge over the A9. At the far end of the bridge turn right and keep walking until you reach a junction: turn left here, towards the hills. Continue on this road, passing beneath the railway line, until you reach another junction immediately following a sharp right turn. Turn left here and carry straight on up the glen of the Coul Burn, keeping to the metalled road.

The road climbs steeply here, up the hillside, past the house of Cloan, terminating at Coulshill Farm. When you reach the road end, continue up the right hand side of the glen on a farm track, which is signposted.

About ½ a mile beyond Coulshill Farm there is a large stand of conifers on the otherwise bare hillside to your right, with a tributary of Coul Burn climbing the hill beyond them. Walk past the trees, turn up the left hand side of the tributary, and follow the track which leads away from it to cross the highest point on the route, in a shallow saddle between two small rounded peaks. From this point the path continues downhill, through the Borland Glen, eventually joining the A823 by the Youth Hostel at the north end of Glendevon village.

If you wish to continue the walk to the town of Dollar (some four miles away), then turn left, towards the village, until you see a signpost for the route to your right. Follow the path across the River Devon and onto the small road on the far side of the glen, then turn right, across a small bridge, and left again, up a steep zig-zagging path, into Glen Quey.

The path is quite clear from here on, and provides an impressive entrance to Dollar, past the dramatic Castle Campbell (open to the public) on its high rock, and down the deep, dark Dollar Glen below it.

8 Blackford to Tillicoultry

Grid Ref: 893 086 (west end of Blackford) **Map Sheet:** 58

A lengthy hill-walk across the Ochil Hills, utilising paths in various stages of decay. Quite gruelling, but offers splendid views of Strathearn and the Grampians at the Blackford end; and of the Forth Valley around Tillicoultry.

Length: 10 miles (one way)
Height Climbed: 1370ft/420m
Grade: A
Public Transport: Regular bus services to and from Blackford and Tillicoultry, with towns linked via Stirling.
Parking: Blackford and Tillicoultry
Toilet Facilities: Blackford and Tillicoultry

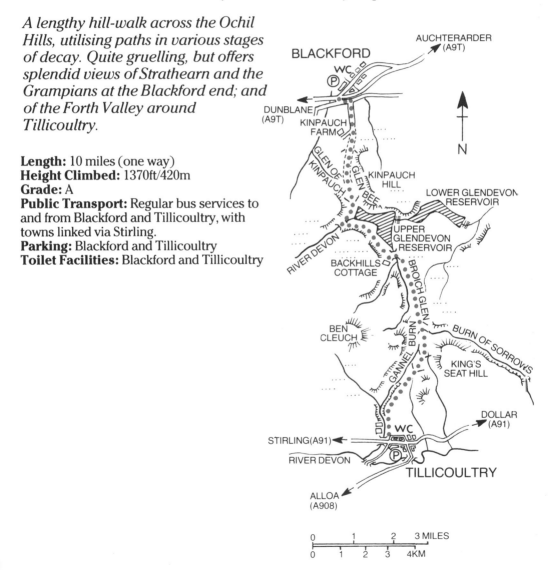

28

This is a lengthy walk, crossing the Ochil range from Strathallan to the Devon Valley. It is steep in places and does offer the opportunity to become lost, so be ready to use your map and compass. The effort is worthwhile, however, since it crosses some splendid countryside and affords marvellous views both north and south.

The route starts from Blackford, a village once burned by the Earl of Mar after the Battle of Sheriffmuir (1715), but now gaining a reputation as the source of Scotland's best-selling mineral water. Leave the village by the south-west end, and walk with care straight across the busy A9(T) to the entrance to a small road directly opposite. Turn left for a short way until you see the sign for Kinpauch Farm. Turn right here, up the drive, being sure to shut the gate behind you.

At the top of the drive, you can pick up a forestry track on the left which leads round the shoulder of Kinpauch Hill - directly before you - and on up the Glen of Kinpauch. The track stops here, but a footpath continues; across a watershed and down Glen Bee towards the Upper Glendevon Reservoir.

Turn right, and follow the path along the hillside above the loch until you reach the bridge across the River Devon, which enters the loch here. Then, turn left, and skirt around Burnfoot Hill, which slopes

steeply into the water, until you pass the cottage of Backhills at the foot of the Broich Glen. Cross the bridge here and walk to the head of the glen up its easterly (left-hand) side.

The path is very vague at this point, and it is important not to cross the burn by mistake and follow either of the tributary glens which enter it from the west (the hill you see above them is Ben Cleuch 2363ft/721m, the highest peak in the Ochil range) but to keep to the **left**-hand side of the glen.

Once you have reached the watershed at the head of Glen Broich, you are at the highest point on the route, on a wide saddle between two low hills. Immediately before you (to the south-east) is King's Seat Hill, and to its left is a deep glen, cut by the Burn of Sorrows which runs down to Dollar. Ignore it, and instead skirt around the low hill to your right, until you can see the deep, narrow glen of the Gannel Burn, which leads down to Tillicoultry.

The path is still vague here, but keep to the easterly (left-hand) side of the glen, and it will gradually become clearer as it passes the deep-set Mill Glen, to your right: a rocky gorge which used to supply power for the mills of Tillicoultry.

The large river on the plain before you is the River Forth, with the town of Alloa on its near bank.

9 *The Oak Walk, Auchterarder*

Grid Ref: 937 123 (bottom of Orchil Rd) **Map Sheet:** 58

A short circular walk, passing through woodland and open farmland, immediately adjacent to Auchterarder.

Length: 2 miles
Height Climbed: Negligible
Grade: C
Public Transport: Regular bus and train services to and from Auchterarder (Gleneagles station).
Parking: In Auchterarder
Toilet Facilities: In Auchterarder

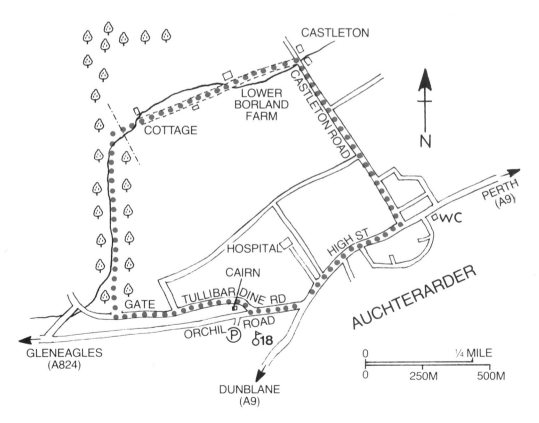

Auchterarder is a long thin town, tucked away under the buttresses of the Ochil Hills on the southern edge of Strathearn. It is probable that it owes its origins to the early Scottish King Malcolm Ceannmor (1052-93) who may have used it as a centre for hunting trips in the area. Since then the town has had a history of fluctuating fortunes, which reached their lowest ebb when it was burned by the Jacobites on their retreat to Perth from Sheriffmuir (1715). The town hit a new peak however in the mid 1800's when Auchterarder became a centre for cloth manufacturing. Knitwear is still produced, but Auchterarder's main source of income is as a service and tourist centre, golf being a particular attraction. Indeed, the famous Gleneagles Hotel (founded by the railway companies in 1924) is just two miles to the west of Auchterarder. The town itself boasts many other smaller, yet excellent hotels, as well as several restaurants and a range of shops, particularly specialising in antiques. Until recently 'The Lang Toon' was straddled by the busy A9, but now the new by-pass makes the High Street a pleasant place for a stroll.

This walk takes you on a loop from the southern end of the town, through some of the surrounding farmland and woodland; partly on surfaced roads, partly on paths and farm tracks.

As you walk south from the centre of the town, turn right, up Orchil Road. Continue up this road until you reach a fork at the cairn erected for Queen Victoria's Silver Jubilee, and then veer right again. Continue along this road until you reach an opening to your right, which leads into a belt of trees. Go through this.

The line of mixed deciduous woodland - with its small burn and multitude of wild flowers during the summer months - runs through cultivated farmland on both sides. Turn right, through a gap in the fence and out of the wood, when you see a small cottage to your left, and a broad farm track leading from it. As you walk along this track - past Lower Borland Farm - you will have a view of the Ochil Hills, over Auchterarder to your right, and of the Grampians rising above Crieff, across Strathearn to your left.

When you reach the end of the track, turn right along the road before you, back into Auchterarder.

Oak

10 Banks of Ericht

Grid Ref: 180 453 (Lower Mill St) **Map Sheet:** 53

A short walk through mixed woodland by the River Ericht, passing the Falls of Ericht and the derelict jute mills which line the river at this point.

Length: 3 miles
Height Climbed: Negligible
Grade: C
Public Transport: Regular bus services to and from Blairgowrie.
Parking: Blairgowrie
Picnic Facilities: Rose gardens
Toilet Facilities: Wellmeadow, Blairgowrie

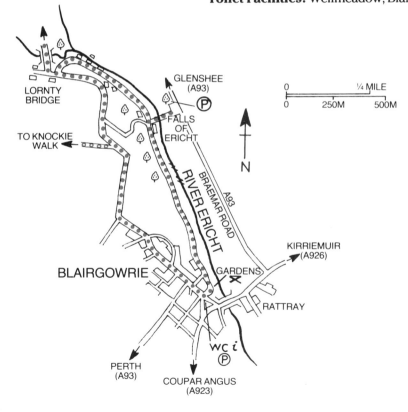

Blairgowrie, now the centre of the soft fruit industry in Strathmore, was once important to the jute industry. Along this route there are a number of old mills - most, sadly, in various stages of dereliction - as well as a selection of mill-lades and weirs, which will be fascinating to anyone interested in industrial history.

Start the walk from the Wellmeadow, and set off down towards the River Ericht along Lower Mill Street; turning left along the river bank by the rose gardens, where the traditional old Mill has been restored and converted to include a restaurant, craft shop and antiques warehouse. Continue along the river bank, through pleasant open woodland, to the Falls of Ericht and Donald Cargill's leap.

Cargill was a local man, and an influential leader of the Covenanters, who was executed in 1681 for opposing the Restoration of the Monarchy. While still on the run he leapt across this point of the River Ericht to escape pursuit - don't be too impressed by the man's prowess, when you see the spot; the river was dynamited and widened by the former Town Council some years ago, partly to help the salmon get up stream against the strong current and partly to stop people from falling in the river while trying to emulate Donald Cargill's feat.

Further upstream you will pass the jute mills at Oakbank. The raw materials for the industry were imported from India, and the reason they found their way to Scotland was largely due to the whaling industry, which had a brief existence on the Scottish east coast during the last century. It was discovered that if the jute was first softened in a mixture of whale oil and water, it could be fed through the machinery which was already used in linen production. The ready supply of whale oil gave the Scottish mills a headstart over the opposition. The jute industry began its steady decline when India began to process its own jute. Please be careful when looking at the old buildings, as they can be dangerous.

Carry on along the river bank until you reach the junction at Lornty Bridge. A short detour to the right will lead you up into the hills and give fine views across Blairgowrie and Strathmore; otherwise, turn left, and the quiet country road will lead you back - past some of the raspberry fields for which the area is famous - to Blairgowrie. This walk may be combined with route no.19, up to the Knockie.

The walk can also be joined from a car park on the A93 Glenshee/Braemar Road. A path leads west from the car park to a new footbridge over the River Ericht which provides good views up and down the river. Adjacent is the restored Keathbank Mill, which houses Scotland's largest working waterwheel.

11 *Cairnwell and Carn Aosda*

Grid Ref: 140 780 (Cairnwell car park) **Map Sheet:** 43

A short, steep hill climb across rough ground, leading to excellent views of the surrounding mountains, with the added attraction of a chair-lift for the less energetic.

Length: 4-6 – miles
Height Climbed: 925ft/283m
Grade: A
Public Transport: None.
Parking: Cairnwell car park
Toilet Facilities: Cairnwell car park

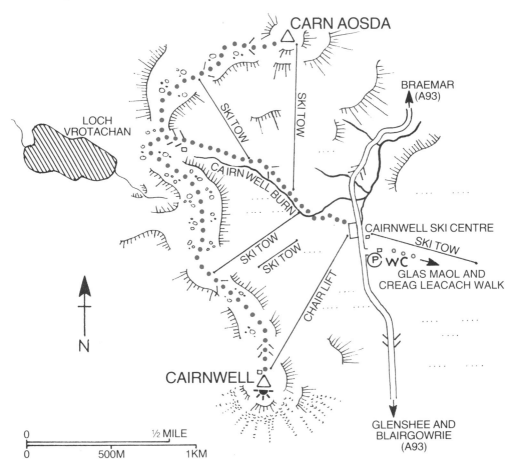

24 miles north of Blairgowrie on the A93 is the Cairnwell Ski Centre (commonly referred to as 'Glenshee', although it is some six miles above the glen). Set in dramatic scenery, and surrounded by some of the highest mountains in Perthshire, this is one of the finest and most popular skiing centres in Scotland, and open hillsides and numerous peaks make it just as attractive to walkers.

Standing in the car park and looking west, a deep corrie can be seen, with a variety of chair-lifts and ski-tows ascending the slopes. On each side of this corrie there is a peak - the one to the left is The Cairnwell (3059ft/933m) while to the right is Carn Aosda (2999ft/917m). To climb these, walk to the back of the Ski Centre buildings, and follow the path leading up the side of the Cairnwell Burn, which drops down the centre of the corrie. After a short but steep climb the path reaches the lowest point on the ridge between the two peaks, and then divides. From here you can turn either right or left - along the broad ridge of chipped stones, heather and dwarf shrubs - to whichever of the two peaks you prefer.

Given a clear day, the views of the surrounding uplands are spectacular, and an indicator on The Cairnwell points out some of the more important peaks which can be seen. While on the tops, look also for ptarmigan, a game bird which is found only above 2000ft, and which has the distinction of turning white during the winter months, to blend in with its surroundings.

In late August and September, these hillsides are also notable for the number of cloudberries to be found.

Return by the same route.

For those who would like to sample the views, but who are not prepared to take on the climb, the chair-lift up The Cairnwell runs for most of the year (with breaks for maintenance at the start and finish of the skiing season) and is a most relaxed and enjoyable way to take in the spectacular Highland scenery. A less relaxed but more exciting way is actually to fly above the hills, and, for the more adventurous, Britains longest established hang-gliding school is situated at the foot of The Cairnwell. Championships are held here in the summer months.

Ptarmigan

12 *Den of Alyth*

Grid Ref: 238 487 (entrance to the den) **Map Sheet:** 53

A series of clear paths set in the wooded glen of the Alyth Burn.

Length: 2½ miles
Height Climbed: Negligible
Grade: C
Public Transport: Regular bus services to and from Alyth.
Parking: Market Square, Alyth, and in the Den.
Toilet Facilities: Alyth
Information Leaflet available from Den of Alyth car park leaflet cairn.

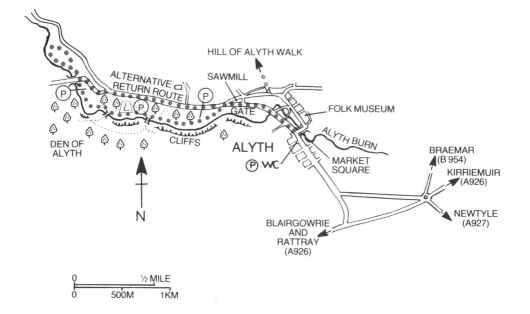

This is a pleasant walk through the deep-set glen of the Alyth Burn, in mixed open woodland which is notable for being naturally seeded and directly descended from the original deciduous woodland which once covered all of lowland Scotland.

To reach Alyth, drive five miles east of Blairgowrie on the A926, before turning left up the A927. The walk starts on the west side of Market Square, leading out of the square up Bamff Road and crossing the Alyth Burn. Stay on this road as it curves to the left, past a large sawmill, before turning left, through the gates of the Den of Alyth ('den' is a word from the Scots dialect signifying a wooded glen). Here, there is a picnic area and climbing fort for children.

The path then runs along the side of the burn, which cuts into the Old Red Sandstone of the district - on the far side of the burn there is a steep cliff face suggesting that the near side of the glen may have subsided at some stage.

Continue up the glen (there are numerous different paths to follow) until you reach a minor road which crosses the burn. The path continues a little further up the glen from the far side of the road.

The nature of woodland - mainly oak and ash with interspersed hazel and wych-elm - provides a habitat for a large number of the smaller woodland birds, while there are dippers and grey wagtails by the water side. Watch also for red squirrels and a wide variety of woodland flowers along the route.

To return to Alyth, either retrace your steps down the den, or follow the minor road back along the edge of the wood, to form a circular route.

The walk may be extended by a stroll around the old streets of the town itself, and a visit to the Folk Museum (see walk no.16).

Red Squirrel

13 *Enochdhu to Kirkmichael*

Grid Ref: 063 627 (Enochdhu) 080 602 (Kirkmichael) **Map Sheet:** 43

A short walk through farmland and forestry linking two settlements in Strath Ardle.

Length: 2 miles (4 miles there and back)
Height Climbed: Negligible
Grade: B
Public Transport: Service bus from Blairgowrie (Glenisla Coaches).
Parking: Small car park at Enochdhu, otherwise use road verges.

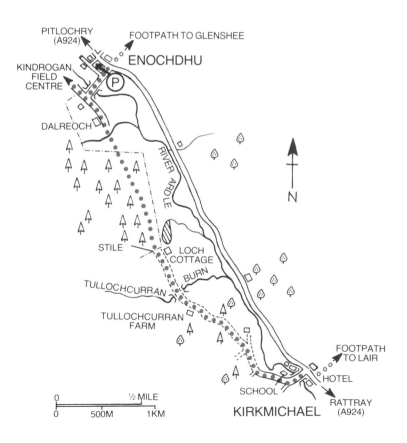

This walk is ideal for anyone who wishes a short breath of east Highland air without having to exert themselves unduly. Parking in the area is a little difficult unfortunately, and some of the paths employed can be muddy when the weather is damp, but the route should pose no difficulties for anyone who is reasonably fit and healthy.

Starting from Kirkmichael, cross the bridge, and turn right beyond the school. Continue along this road (which soon becomes a track), out of the housing and along the path above the River Ardle. At one point the path divides: continue along the left hand route, past Tullochcurran farm, over Tullochcurran Burn and on to Loch Cottage, on the side of a small lochan on the edge of Kindrogan Wood. The path passes to the left of the cottage, and crosses a stile into the wood, which is a Forestry Commission conifer plantation.

In a short distance the path emerges from the wood and passes Dalreoch Farm before splitting once again. If you take the left fork you will reach the Kindrogan Field Centre where information is available (in the booklets which accompany their forest walks) on the history of the area. If you turn right at the junction, you will recross the River Ardle and find yourself in the small collection of houses known as Enochdhu.

While on this walk watch for roe deer and red squirrels, and also for black grouse, pheasants and capercaillies, the largest species of birds resident in the Perthshire pine forests.

Capercaillies require large areas of pine forest to survive, with heather and shrub cover on the forest floor. As the Highlands were deforested in the 17th and 18th centuries, the capercaillies were gradually exterminated. However, 55 of the birds were brought back into Scotland from Sweden in 1830 by the Marquis of Breadalbane and the bird has become re-established in the 20th century with the replanting of coniferous forests.

For anyone looking for a much longer walk, this path can be used as a connecting section for a round walk from Glenshee (see the 'Kirkmichael to Lair' and 'Enochdhu to Spittal of Glenshee' walks) which would total around 17 miles, including a stretch on the A93.

Capercaillie (Female)   *(Male)*

14 *Enochdhu to Spittal of Glenshee*

Grid Ref: 063 627 (Enochdhu); 110 699 (Spittal of Glenshee) **Map Sheet:** 43

A stiff walk, largely along good paths, crossing the high moorland between the valleys of the Ardle and the Shee Water.

Length: 6 miles
Height Climbed: 1300ft/400m
Grade: A/B
Public Transport: Service bus from Blairgowrie to Enochdhu (Glenisla Coaches).
Parking: Enochdhu – on opposite side of road from walk-end; Spittal of Glenshee Hotel

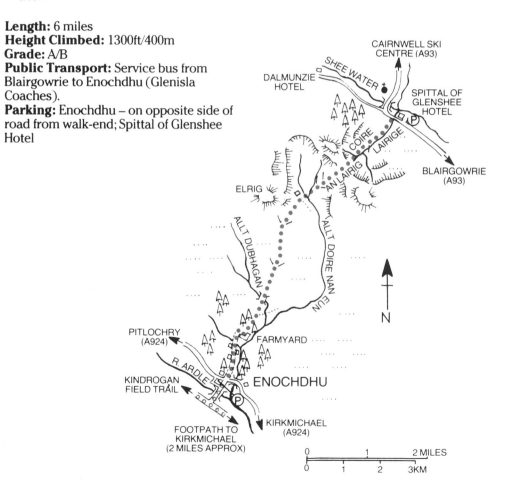

This path crosses the high land between the valleys of Strathardle and Glenshee, connecting by a direct route the two settlements of Enochdhu (15 miles north of Blairgowrie and nine miles east of Pitlochry on the A924) and Spittal of Glenshee (19 miles north of Blairgowrie on the A93).

Starting from Enochdhu, look for the start of the route - a signposted path leading from the road into a stand of conifers - and park your car inside the farmyard opposite. The path leads up a slope, past a number of houses, before entering a farmyard; turn left here, and follow the track as it heads off through another stand of trees, before continuing to rise across open grass and moorland. 1½ miles from the start of the walk the path splits; follow the left hand branch, across the bridge over the Allt Dubhagan, and on past the conical peak of Elrig. Just beyond this hill the path begins to climb in earnest: crossing the Allt Doire nan Eun and heading for a saddle between two hills at the head of the glen - An Lairig (2133ft/650m) - the highest point on the walk.

From this saddle there are fine views, particularly eastwards: across Glenshee, and up Gleann Beag on the far side, towards the ski slopes on the Cairnwell.

The remainder of the walk is a swift descent of the grassy slopes of the corrie before you (Coire Lairige), leading down to the Spittal of Glenshee Hotel, by the roadside below.

You can return by the same route, but for those who are interested in a longer walk, a round route of some 17 miles can be made if this walk is joined with the 'Enochdhu to Kirkmichael' and 'Kirkmichael to Lair' routes, which can be found elsewhere in this book (Routes 13 and 18).

Whilst crossing the hills, watch out for the blue hare - quite common in this part of the Highlands - which turns white during the winter to camouflage itself against the snow. You might also catch sight of deer (red and roe) and both black and red grouse.

Red Deer Stag

15 *Glas Maol and Creag Leacach*

Grid Ref: 140 780 (Cairnwell car park) **Map Sheet:** 43

A brisk, steep hill climb, across rough ground, leading to excellent views of the surrounding mountains.

Length: 7 miles
Height Climbed: 1400ft/420m (with undulations)
Grade: A
Public Transport: None.
Parking: Cairnwell car park
Toilet Facilities: Cairnwell car park

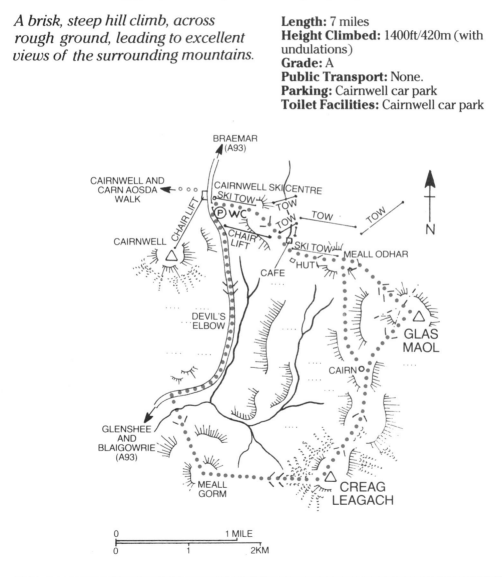

To reach this walk, follow the A93 for 24 miles north from Blairgowrie - through Glenshee and Gleann Beag - until you reach the car park at the Cairnwell Ski Centre. Most of the ski slopes are to the west of the road, on the slopes of The Cairnwell and Carn Aosda, but this path leads up the eastern side of the glen (where skiing facilities have been extended in recent years).

Starting from the car park, the path is vague at first, and very steep in places, but the first checkpoint is easily found - the peak of Meall Odhar (3025ft/922m) at the end of the north-western ridge of Glas Maol, jutting out above the ski slopes. From here the path drops to cross a narrow col between two deep corries, before rising steeply once again to reach the broad rounded summit of Glas Maol (3504ft/1068m), from where the views of the surrounding mountains are superb, as you would expect. Look also for the remains of three old fences which meet just short of the top: these mark the boundaries of the old counties of Perthshire, Aberdeenshire and Angus.

To continue the route, walk south-west, following the narrow, scree-coated ridge of Creag Leacach (3238ft/987m) to its peak. From here there are three options for the return route to the car park: firstly, you could return by the route you came; secondly, you could continue to the most southerly point on the ridge, and carefully descend across the scree on the north-west slope, heading towards Meall Gorm (2490ft/759m), and from there return to the road - this route involves a walk of 1½

miles along the A93, however, which you may wish to avoid. Thirdly, you could return along the ridge of Creag Leacach until you reached the cairn (one mile from the peak), and from there skirt around the edge of Glas Maol, to rejoin the path followed on the ascent at Meall Odhar.

Because of the height of the road above sea-level at this point (2149ft/655m), Glas Maol and The Cairnwell (on the opposite side of the glen) are two of the easiest Munros (peaks above 3000ft) to climb in Perthshire, and offer an opportunity to sample the beauties of the mountain tops without undergoing the usual lengthy trek to do so. By the same token, the sensitive ecology of the peaks is under more pressure than that of other, less accessible hills, and you are particularly asked not to disturb the flora and fauna of the area more than is absolutely necessary. Both Glas Maol and Creag Leacach fall within the Caenlochan National Nature Reserve.

Black Grouse
(Female)   (Male)

16 *Hill of Alyth*

Grid Ref: 244 488 (start of walk) **Map Sheet:** 53

A brisk hill walk giving good views of Strathmore. Mostly on farm tracks and across the open hill, with a connecting section along a metalled road, and a possible extension over Balduff Hill.

Length: 5 miles (with an extra 9 miles is Balduff Hill is included)
Height Climbed: 570ft/170m
Grade: B
Public Transport: Regular bus services to and from Alyth
Parking: Market Sq, Alyth
Toilet Facilities: Alyth

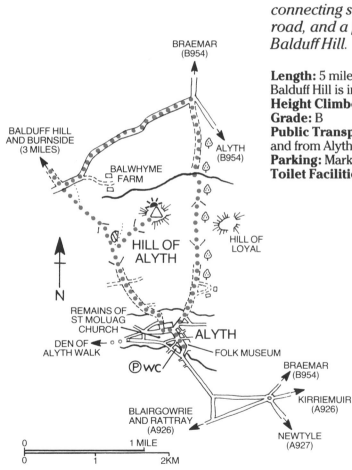

Alyth, five miles east of Blairgowrie on the A926, is a small market town, situated on the Highland Line, with the Hill of Alyth to the north, the Grampians to the west, the wide fertile plain of Strathmore to the south and the Sidlaw Hills running parallel to the Highland Line on the far side of the strath. This walk takes you from the Market Square in the centre of Alyth, over the Hill of Alyth - giving fine views on the way - and back by a different route.

Starting from Commercial Street - on the east side of the Alyth Burn - walk north, continuing up the hill on Toutie Street, so called because of the noise of the herd-boy's horn as he took the cattle to graze on the hill in days gone by. When you reach the junction at the top of the street, turn left along High Street. On your left stand the three recently restored and floodlit arches of the Medieval church, St Moluag.

A short way along High Street turn right, through a gap between the houses, and continue along the farm track before you, which is signposted as a footpath to Burnside. Follow this path up the hill - crossing a junction with another track and heading north, for the ridge of the hill.

Once at the highest point of the path, make a detour to the right, on to the summit of the hill and admire the superb panoramic views of the surrounding countryside.

The top of the hill is criss-crossed with paths, and can be a little confusing, but if you take the path to the left of the small lochan, which is at the highest point of the path, and aim to the left of Balwhyme Farm at the roadside below, you cannot go far wrong. Once on the road you have the option of a walk to Burnside, on the far side of the hill ahead (Balduff Hill). If you follow this path and return to Alyth (either by the same route or by road) it will add about nine miles to the length of the walk.

Otherwise, turn right, along the metalled road, to the junction with the B954. Here, a path leads up the slope to your right, between the Hill of Alyth and the Hill of Loyal. This broad elegant route was once a road of some importance, and is lined, along one side, by a splendid row of trees. It leads you straight back to Alyth (turn right for the junction at the head of Toutie Street where you may wish to visit the Folk Museum in Commercial Street. The museum outlines the history of the town, including a number of fascinating exhibits relating to farm life).

Alyth still retains the relaxed and friendly atmosphere of a traditional Scottish farming town. The Agricultural Show, held at the end of June, is one of the largest in the area, and well worth a visit.

17 *Kindrogan Hill Trail*

Grid Ref: 054 629 (Kindrogan Field Centre) **Map Sheet:** 43

A well signposted forest walk which leads through dense woodland to fine views from the peak of Kindrogan Hill.

Length: 3½ miles
Height Climbed: 800ft/245m
Grade: B
Public Transport: Service bus from Blairgowrie (Glenisla Coaches)
Parking: Kindrogan Field Centre
Toilet Facilities: None
Information Leaflet available from Field Centre

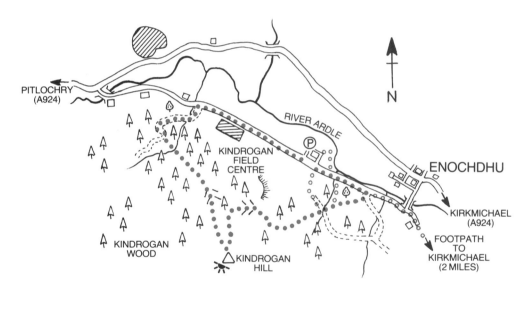

The Kindrogan Field Centre, situated in Strath Ardle, 10 miles from Pitlochry on the A924 road for Bridge of Cally and Blairgowrie, is a residential centre, maintained by the Scottish Field Studies Association and partly financed by the Scottish Education Department and other bodies. Its objectives are to promote all branches of field studies (archaeology, natural history, geology etc) and to this end it runs a number of courses during the year.

In addition to these activities the centre also maintains a nature trail; an accompanying booklet, explaining points of interest along the route, is available from the main building.

To reach the centre, cross the River Ardle at Enochdhu, a tiny hamlet typical of those found throughout Perthshire. The drive is signposted for the centre.

The walk begins at the Lodge House before the centre, and leads steeply up the side of Kindrogan Hill - through dense, coniferous, Forestry Commission woodland - to the open summit of the hill. The lack of trees allows for fine views in all directions, and a viewfinder in the trail guide names all the major peaks which are visible, including Beinn a' Ghlo, Ben Vrackie and the Sidlaw Hills to the south-east.

From the hill top the path continues northward, down through the wood to rejoin the road to the Field Centre. Turn right here for ½ mile to return to the car park.

This is a pleasant forest walk, and offers an opportunity to see such wildlife as red squirrels, roe deer (or even red deer in the winter months) pheasants and goldcrests. If the hill climb is a little too much for you, there is an alternative, shorter, low-level route around the Field Centre, for which a booklet is also available.

Roe Deer Buck

18 *Kirkmichael to Lair (Glenshee)*

Grid Ref: 081 602 (Kirkmichael end of walk) 142 634 (Lair) **Map Sheet:** 43

A brisk hill walk along largely unreliable tracks, through some fine rolling hill land, typical of the scenery of the eastern highlands.

Length: 5 miles (one way)
Height Climbed: 590ft/179m (with undulations)
Grade: B
Public Transport: Mail bus along Glenshee; service bus to Kirkmichael from Blairgowrie (Glenisla Coaches)
Parking: Very limited; road verges, Kirkmichael etc
Toilet Facilities: Kirkmichael

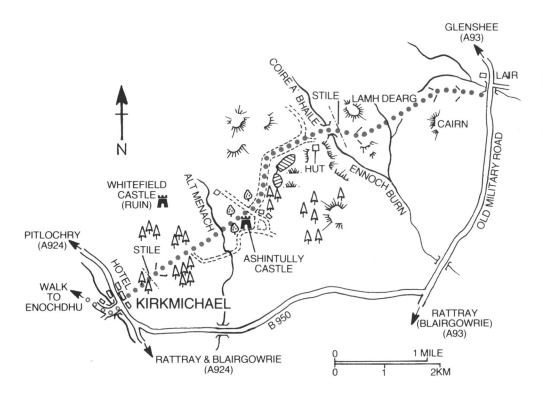

In the eastern highlands of Perthshire and Angus, as the Grampian range nears the Highland Boundary Fault, the geography of the region takes on a distinctive character, with high, undulating table lands, dissected by a series of deep, flat-bottomed glaciated valleys, whose rivers, notably the Tay, flow out on to the low, fertile farmland of Strathmore. This walk crosses the high ground between two such valleys.

Kirkmichael is a small village situated in Strath Ardle; some 12 miles east of Pitlochry on the A924, and a similar distance north of Blairgowrie. The path to follow is signposted to one side of the Kirkmichael Hotel on the main street.

At first the path is easily followed, but it quickly becomes less clear, and you will need to make sure of reaching Glenshee by the most direct route. After leaving Kirkmichael, it follows field boundaries until it reaches a small stand of conifers and crosses the last fence by a stile. Before you, there is now a wide stretch of grassland, on a gradual incline, with no obvious path in sight. To stay on route, look for the three stands of conifer trees at the top of the hill ahead, and set a course to pass just to the left of the right hand group.

When you have reached the far end of this stand of trees, you will see a farm track which cuts hard right before turning towards a number of buildings (including Ashintully Castle, a large house built around an original 16th century tower) in a group of trees. Ignore this track, and head straight across the wide glen of Allt Menach before you, aiming to the left of the castle. If you look to your left at this point you will see the ruins of another old 16th century keep, Whitefield Castle, overlooking the glen.

Once you are beyond Ashintully you will join a farm track which passes to the left of two small lochans, before splitting in two directions. Follow the right-hand track, which leads to a small hut on a hill above Coire a'Bhaile, the upper glen of the Ennoch Burn. Across the burn below there is a footbridge, with a stile over the fence beyond it.

Once you have crossed both of these, look up the slope in front and to the right and you should see a wooden post with a yellow top. This is one of the waymarks which will now lead you around the spur of the hill; across the watershed between Lamh Dearg and Cairn, and down alongside the burn to Lair, joining the A93 through Glenshee. Be prepared to navigate yourself, however, as these posts are occasionally uprooted, either by cattle or by the weather.

Blairgowrie is 13 miles south on the A93, which was originally built in the 18th century as a military road.

19 *The Knockie*

Grid Ref: 176 451 (foot of Newton Street) **Map Sheet:** 53

A walk which takes you through the outskirts of Blairgowrie on metalled roads, and through the surrounding farmlands (largely fruit-growing) on various paths and farm tracks.

Length: 5 miles
Height Climbed: 438ft/134m
Grade: B
Public Transport: Regular bus services to and from Blairgowrie
Parking: In Blairgowrie
Toilet Facilities: Wellmeadow, Blairgowrie

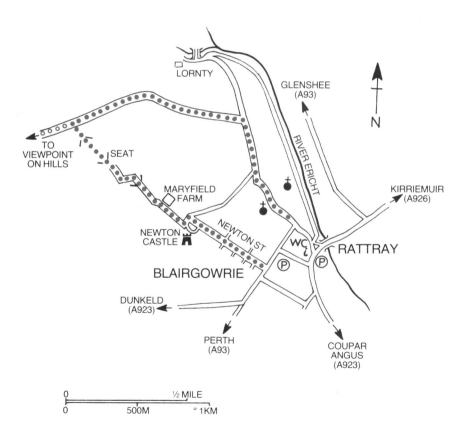

Blairgowrie, which forms a single burgh with the town of Rattray on the opposite side of the River Ericht, is the focal point of Strathmore's fruit-growing industry. It is particularly famous for raspberries, which grow on the fertile red loams of the sunny south-facing slopes around the town. It was in the 1890's that James Mackenzie Hodge, a local solicitor, noticed the quality of the local wild raspberries and the favourable growing conditions, and initiated the planting out of the canes. The landscape was gradually transformed, and many thousands of folk from Central Scotland have since travelled to summer camps in the area to help with the berry harvest.

This walk takes you through the outskirts of the town, and on up the Knockie; a small hill which is in fact, the last foot hill of the Grampian range at this point on the Highland Line.

The path starts as Newton Street, which turns up the hill from the A93 road to Perth. Carry straight on up this street before turning left where the houses end, just beyond Newton Castle, a large, white, 16th century building which is the home of the Chief of the Clan Macpherson.

Beyond the castle, a track leads straight up the hill, in between fields, passing close by Maryfield Farm. Beyond this, near the top of the hill, there is a seat where you can enjoy the splendid views of Strathmore, and beyond that again there is an indicator, naming some of the more important points in the landscape, such as the Sidlaw Hills, across the valley to the south-east.

The path becomes a little narrower (and muddier, when damp) for a while, until it reaches a junction at a surfaced road. If you turn left here for a short way, you will be rewarded with some fine views of the hills above Dunkeld, but to continue the walk, turn right, passing between fields once again for about a mile, until you reach the road from Blairgowrie to Lornty Bridge. Turn right here and continue down this road, with the River Ericht at the foot of the slope to your left, until you re-enter Blairgowrie. Alternatively, turn left to Lornty Bridge and return to the town via the Banks of the Ericht (see route No.10).

Rowan (Mountain Ash)

20 Ben Vorlich

Grid Ref: 633 233 (Eastern gateway to Ardvorlich House) **Map Sheets:** 51 and 57

A steep hill climb, along rough tracks and over various ground conditions – soft peat to hard rock – leading to fine views from the summit, and a possible extension to Stuc a' Chroin.

Length: 7 – 9 miles
Height Climbed: 2870ft/878m
Grade: A
Public Transport: None (buses to and from St Fillans from Crieff and Perth).
Parking: By roadside
Toilet Facilities: None

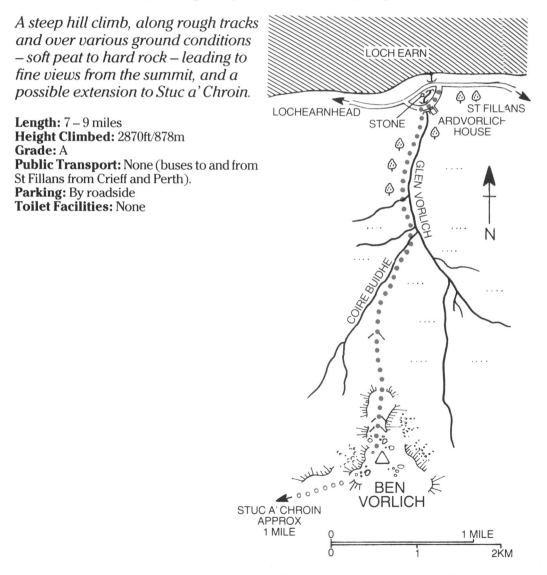

Ben Vorlich is a steep-sided, shapely hill with twin peaks which rises to a height of 3224ft/985m from the southern side of Loch Earn. Its undoubted popularity amoung hillwalkers results partly from its accessible situation in south-western Perthshire, and its pyramidal summit which is a distinctive feature of the skyline at many points between Perth and Stirling. The route to the summit is obvious, and not dangerous in good weather conditions, yet it presents sufficient difficulty to leave the walker with a feeling of achievement.

To reach the start of the walk, drive along the south side of Loch Earn, and park in the lay-bys provided. near the entrance to Ardvorlich House (five miles from St Fillans and four miles from Lochearnhead). The route leads up the drive to the house (there are two drives at Ardvorlich; walkers are asked to use the easterly entrance, ie the one nearest St Fillans). Before starting up the drive, you may wish to visit the spot by the side of the road - on the other side of the bridge over the Vorlich Burn - near where are 'interred the bodies of seven McDonalds of Glencoe', the victims of retaliation to a McDonald raid by the people of Ardvorlich in 1620. The grave was rediscovered in the last century and a stone erected to mark the spot; an interesting reminder of less peaceful times on Loch Earn-side.

Walk up the drive and turn right, towards the house, across the Vorlich burn, before turning sharp left again, through a small gate and on up Glen Vorlich.

The path is good here, and after about one mile it forks. Follow the right hand path, which leads up into Coire Buidhe, and then onto the broad ridge of Ben Vorlich which juts out due north from the summit. Follow this ridge to the top of the hill, being careful of the steep, rocky section near the summit.

Those who are more experienced at hill walking may now wish to extend the walk to include the peak of Stuc a' Chroin (3178ft/972m) to the south-west of Ben Vorlich, across a deep col. When climbing the steep ascent on the far side of the col, keep to the right of the crest, avoiding the worst of the broken rocks around the peak. This is a hard walk, care should be taken especially in winter.

The views from Ben Vorlich are excellent: north to Ben Lawers, west to Ben More and Stob Binnein above Glen Dochart, and south towards the lowlands, including Stirling Castle and Arthur's Seat in Edinburgh.

Return by the same route.

21 *Crieff Nature Trail*

Grid Ref: 861 234 (Culcrieff Farm) **Map Sheet:** 52

A short nature trail with an accompanying descriptive map, through the woodland and farmland to the north of Crieff.

Length: 1½ miles (2 miles including return to Culcrieff Farm)
Height Climbed: Negligible
Grade: C
Public Transport: Regular bus services to and from Crieff.
Parking: Crieff or Culcrieff Farm
Toilet Facilities: Crieff (James Sq)
Descriptive Map: available from Crieff Tourist Information Centre.

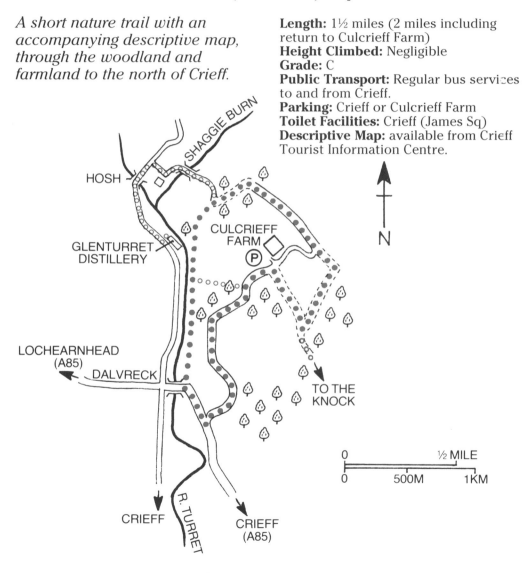

The Crieff Nature Trail - which starts about ½ mile north of Crieff - has been prepared by members of the Scottish Wildlife Trust (in association with the Crieff Hydro Hotel, on whose land the trail is situated). If walked using the descriptive map as reference (available from the Tourist Information Centre in High Street) it gives an excellent introduction to the flora and fauna of the district, as well as explaining the geology of the area, and the natural forces which have helped to shape the landscape.

The trail starts from Culcrieff Farm, and to reach this by car you should head north-west along the A85 road to Lochearnhead, and turn right just outside Crieff, along a small road: this leads directly to a car park at Culcrieff Farm. Alternatively, you can walk to the farm from Crieff, around the foot of the Knock (see map).

The walk starts off heading south from the farm, before cutting back northwards after a short distance, and looping round behind Culcrieff to drop down to the banks of the River Turret.

Along the route there are eight numbered posts, which correspond to extensive notes on the descriptive map explaining the points of interest in the immediate vicinity. By following these numbered posts, an exit point will be reached on the farm road just short of the Steading.

The path passes through a number of different natural environments: cultivated farmland; the banks of the River Turret;

and a variety of types of woodland - mainly oak, beech and birch, but with an added selection of ash, alder, chestnut and others. The observant walker may see some mammals on the route, such as roe deer and grey squirrels (which were first introduced into Britain from North America in 1876, and are gradually replacing the native red squirrels, although the red variety is still common north of the Highland line).

The bird life includes curlews, oystercatchers, sand martins, dippers and a variety of tits and finches, while there is a bewildering array of wild flowers, lichens and fungi, all of which are indicated along the route.

At the most northern point of the walk, a short detour over the footbridge at Shaggie Burn and the Hosh road bridge leads walkers to Glenturret Distillery where a guided tour and excellent meal can be enjoyed.

This walk makes an ideal short outing which may be combined with visits to the distillery and craft workshops in Crieff, to provide a varied day out.

Silver Birch

22 *Glen Lednock Circular Walk*

Grid Ref: 773 222 (Comrie car park) **Map Sheet:** 51 or 52

A signposted route through woodland and farmland in a particularly pleasant glen. On the route there is a large waterfall, and extensive views from Lord Melville's Monument.

Length: 4 miles
Height Climbed: 640ft/200m
Grade: B
Public Transport: Bus service to Comrie from Crieff, Perth and St Fillans
Parking: Comrie
Toilet Facilities: Comrie
Information Leaflet available from Laggan Car Park and Crieff Tourist Information Centre

Comrie is a pleasant village in upper Strathearn, lying six miles west of Crieff on the A85. The name comes from the Gaelic word 'combruith' - signifying a confluence of rivers - and indeed, three separate rivers merge at this point: the Earn, the Ruchill Water, and the Lednock. This walk takes you up the glen of the Lednock.

Start at Laggan car park at the east end of Comrie where there is a leaflet cairn. The leaflet will prove a useful guide and will lead you across the Lednock to Comrie School. Turn right beyond the school, carry straight on to Monument Road and turn right at the sign of the Circular Walk. This leads you to a path through the wood.

Continue along this path, through woods of beech, oak and larch, making a detour to the right to view the Wee Cauldron - a set of rapids - before continuing upstream to the Deil's Cauldron. A long flight of steps leads down the steep side of the glen to a viewpoint, where the power of the water can be seen at close proximity as it rushes through its dark gully.

The path now joins the metalled road up the glen for a short distance, before making another optional detour, this time up the hill to the left - Dun More - to visit the 72ft/22m high monument which was erected there in 1812, in memory of Henry Dundas, the 1st Viscount Melville. The path is steep, but the magnificent views from the summit more than justify the effort: over the cliffs to the south (be careful of these) Comrie can be seen below, with Strathearn widening to the east, and the peaks of the Ochils and the Lomonds in the distance. To the north is upper Glen Lednock, with the summit of Ben Chonzie (3048ft/929m) behind it; while, to the west, the River Earn flows down from Loch Earn, with the peak of Ben Vorlich (3224ft/985m) visible to the left of the loch.

Return to the road and follow the signposts for 'Laggan Wood', crossing the Lednock by the ingenious Shaky Bridge, one end of which is balanced in the fork of a sycamore. In the field to the right of the path, just before the bridge, is a large mound encircled by a row of oaks and spanish chestnuts. This is believed to have been, at one time, the site of a chapel.

The path follows the river for a short distance, as it winds through open fields, before gently climbing the slope above the river, and entering Laggan Wood over a stile. The wood is a mixture of planted conifer trees, and self-set birch and oaks - particularly evident in the deep river gully to the right of the path.

Follow the path through the wood until it re-enters Comrie. Turn left to return to the car park. While in the locality, you may wish to visit Auchingarrich Wildlife Centre (2 miles south of the village) and Drummond Fish Farm (to the west of the village).

23 *The Knock*

Grid Ref: 864 216 (James Square) **Map Sheet:** 52

A short, steep walk from the centre of Crieff, through largely deciduous woods, to a viewpoint on the Knock.

Length: 3 miles
Height Climbed: 650ft/200m
Grade: B
Public Transport: Regular bus services to and from Crieff
Parking: Crieff and The Knock
Toilet Facilities: Crieff (James Square)

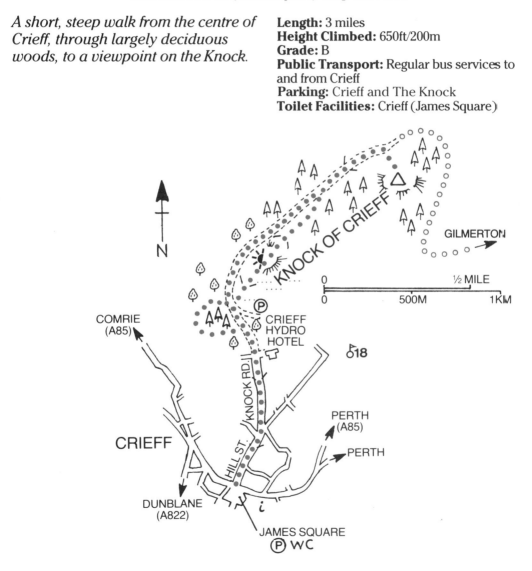

Crieff, like all the towns which lie along the Highland Line, held an uneasy position as a meeting place of the Gaelic and Lowland cultures. Throughout the 16th and 17th centuries it was famed as the location for the annual 'Michaelmas Tryst', when the Highlanders brought their cattle from the north to sell to the Lowland and English buyers; a great occasion at its height, when over 30,000 cattle were sold each year. The town was also the seat of justice for the region, and many Highland cattle-thieves ended their days on the 'Kind Gallows' of Crieff. Perhaps the Highlanders bore this in mind when the Jacobite army burned the town to the last house (as they burned so much of Strathearn) during the first rising in 1716.

Crieff - a little quieter these days - lies back against a large mound of tree-covered old red sandstone, known as the 'Knock of Crieff', and a walk to the top, to sample the view, is well worth the effort.

Start from James Square (set out by James Drummond, the 3rd Duke of Perth, when the town was being rebuilt in 1731) and follow the signpost up Hill Street. Veer left up Knock Road, and follow this road until it passes through a gate and becomes a wide track. To your right at this point is the Crieff Hydro Hotel; a reminder of Crieff's vogue, in the 19th century, as a spa and health resort. At the back of the Hydro's chalets is a public car park. Climb the second path to the left of the car park to reach the lower summit of 'The Knock'. This path leads directly uphill, and is crossed by other paths which may be explored on another visit. The main route to the lower summit leads through the trees onto open hillside. At the summit there is a Cradle Stone and a view indicator which identifies the hills and towns to the south, the east and the Grampian Mountains to the north.

The path now continues along the ridge and turns left to join a forest road. The main route continues uphill: downhill leads back to the car park.

Heading uphill, the Upper Knock (911ft/278m) is passed to the right and to the left, further on, is a division which provides views over Monzie Castle to the hills beyond. The forest road now bends back on itself passing by the ruins of Ferntower House. Here the path to Gilmerton is signposted. Keep on the forest road to return to the back of the Hydro's chalets near the car park.

24 *Lady Mary's Walk*

Grid Ref: 864 215 (James Square) **Map Sheet:** 52

A leisurely walk along the north bank of the River Earn, and back to Crieff along farm tracks and metalled roads.

Length: 3 miles
Height Climbed: Negligible
Grade: C
Public Transport: Regular bus services to and from Crieff
Parking: Taylor Park
Picnic Site: Taylor Park
Toilet Facilities: James Square

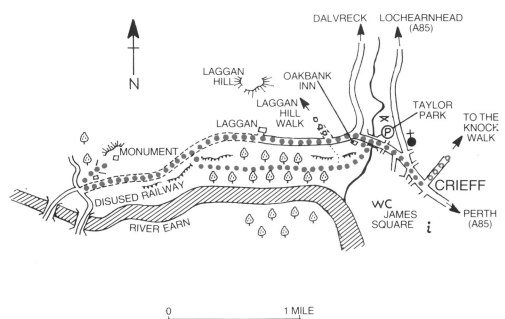

Lady Mary's Walk was created in around 1815 by the laird of Ochtertyre, and was the favourite walk of his daughter, Lady Mary Murray. It is still just as popular today, and provides the opportunity for a leisurely wander by the banks of the peaceful River Earn, as it flows past Crieff on its route from Loch Earn to the Firth of Tay.

If starting the walk from James Square, head west by following the road signs for Comrie. At the War Memorial turn left downhill to join Milnab Street and continue on to Taylor Park.

From Taylor Park, where there is a public car park, cross the River Turret by the road bridge. Turn left at the far end of the bridge and follow the path as it leads down the side of the Turret, before turning right along the banks of the River Earn. The embankment to your right is all that remains of the railway line which used to continue up the valley to Loch Earn and beyond. The path stays close to the river for about a mile, and remains clear and flat, with some fine beech and Scots pine trees lining the early part of the route.

When this riverside section peters out turn right, through a gap in the old railway embankment, and you will find yourself on a well used farm track. Up to your left, on a low, wooded hill, you can see the obelisk monument, this was erected in memory of Sir David Baird, a general who particularly distinguished himself in India at the close of the 18th century. If you turn left the path will ultimately lead you to the monument, which is about a mile away. Otherwise,

turn right and follow the track to Oakbank, where an old tree called 'Eppie Calims Oak' stands at the corner of the road.

From here it is a short walk downhill to where you started your walk along the banks of the Turret.

While on the banks of the Earn, watch particularly for birds associated with the water: herons, oystercatchers, grey wagtails, dippers and ducks.

This walk also gives you the opportunity to relax and enjoy the delightful trees, flowerbeds and shrubs of Taylor Park and the adjacent, larger, MacRosty Park, given to the town by a former Provost. The two are separated by an old mill stream, and facilities include putting, tennis, trampolining and children's playgrounds for those with the energy to spare.

Old Scots Pine

25 Laggan Hill

Grid Ref: 858 221 (car park in Taylor Park) **Map Sheet:** 52

A pleasant path through farmland and woodland, across a low hill to the west of Crieff.

Length: 2½ miles (one way)
Height Climbed: 360ft/110m
Grade: C
Public Transport: Regular bus services to and from Crieff
Parking: Taylor Park car park; Crieff
Picnic Site: Taylor Park
Toilet Facilities: Crieff, James Square

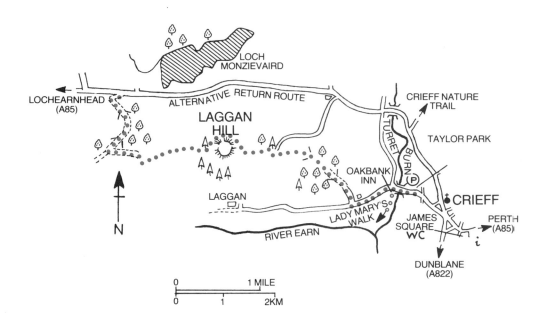

Laggan Hill is a small rounded prominence, rising to the west of Crieff, to a height of only 515ft/156m. This walk crosses the hill, from the outskirts of Crieff to a meeting with the A85 road, where it passes Loch Monzievaird.

To reach the start of the walk, leave Crieff along the minor road which cuts through Taylor Park before crossing the River Turret (see Route 24 'Lady Mary's Walk' for the path to Taylor Park). Once across the river, turn left beyond the Oakbank Inn, and continue along the minor road for ¼ mile, before turning right up a straight drive beyond a small house to the right of the road.

The path is quite clear from now on, as it leads through farmland at first, before passing into a fine, mixed deciduous wood. It then continues along the ridge of the hill, now and again providing views across the Earn Valley below, as it moves through open farmland - banked by drystane dykes and lines of trees - on its passage from wood to wood: some deciduous, some conifer plantations. The path continues over a stile and through overgrown woodland for about ⅓ mile.

There are two junctions along the route (see map). Continue straight on at the first, ignoring the farm track leading off to the right, and turn right at the second - on the edge of a large wood, near the Monzievaird end of the path.

The mixture of woodland and farmland along this route provides for a fine selection of bird life: in the woods there are a great many tits, finches and wood pigeons, while the fields - at different times in the year - play host to oystercatchers, curlews and lapwings among others. Watch also for waterfowl on the small, weedy lochan near the crest of the hill, where herons may even be seen.

To return to Crieff, turn back along the route you came. It is not recommended that walkers use the main A85, as it is a busy road without a proper footpath.

Beech

26 Around Birnam

Grid Ref: 027 424 (Dunkeld Bridge) **Map Sheet:** 52 or 53

A system of short walks encompassing the town of Birnam and its surrounding fields, and river banks, forming part of the fully waymarked Dunkeld and Birnam Walks System.

Length: 2 – 4 miles
Height Climbed: Negligible
Grade: C
Public Transport: Regular bus and train services to and from Dunkeld and Birnam
Parking: Car park in Dunkeld and Birnam
Picnic Site: Jubilee Park, first right past Birnam Oak
Toilet Facilities: In Birnam
Information Leaflet: Available at Dunkeld Tourist Information Centre.

DUNKELD

INVER (HERMITAGE WALK)

STEPS

LITTLE DUNKELD

PITLOCHRY (A9)

WC

BIRNAM OAK

N

RIVER TAY

PLAY AREA

BIRNAM

BEATRIX POTTER GARDEN

INCHEWAN BURN

STATION

0   ¼ MILE
0   250M   500M

PERTH (A9)

BIRNAM HILL WALK

Birnam is a relatively modern town; and came into being largely because the railway builders of the 19th century elected to build their line on the opposite side of the River Tay from the more ancient settlement of Dunkeld. The town which subsequently grew up around the station displays characteristic late Victorian architecture, but its name holds a place in the popular imagination because of Shakespeare's play 'Macbeth':

> 'Macbeth shall never vanquished be, until Great Birnam wood to high Dunsinaine hill Shall come against him.'

How historically accurate the play is it is impossible to guess, but on this walk there is at least one link with the 11th century, when the real Macbeth was still living in this part of the world.

Start walking from the southern end of Dunkeld Bridge, follow the steps down to the river bank and turn right. The first part of the walk is flanked by buildings, but these quickly end and, once you have crossed the Inchewan Burn, you will find the most famous object on this part of the river: the Birnam Oak. It is uncertain just how old the tree is, but if indeed Malcolm stripped branches from the trees of Birnam Wood to camouflage his army on the march to Dunsinaine, this oak could certainly have been used for the purpose. Look also for a particularly old sycamore tree just beside it.

Opposite the oak there is a children's play area - to the right of the path - and beyond that the path continues with fields on your right and a line of large beech trees fringing the river to your left. Presently, the path doubles back to join the main road back into Birnam Hotel. You can visit the popular and fun Beatrix Potter theme garden; a tribute to Birnam's most famous and well-loved early visitor. As well as the garden's interpretation pavilion and planting, there are the exquisite bronze sculptures of all Beatrix's best-known animal characters.

There is also an alternative path - if you turn left at the foot of the Dunkeld Bridge steps - which ultimately leads to the village of Inver on the River Braan (¾ mile) and beyond that to the Hermitage Walk. Inver was the birthplace, in 1727, of Niel Gow, perhaps the most famous of Scottish fiddlers, and his cottage may still be seen.

This walk forms part of the much larger, fully waymarked Dunkeld and Birnam Walks System (see also Walks 27 & 29 in this book).

Sycamore

27 *Birnam Hill*

Grid Ref: 027 424 (Dunkeld Bridge) **Map Sheets:** 52 or 53

A steep hill walk through varied woodland and across open moorland, with excellent views, forming part of the fully waymarked Dunkeld and Birnam Walks System.

Length: 4 – 6 miles
Height Climbed: 1120ft/343m
Grade: B
Public Transport: Regular bus and train services to and from Dunkeld and Birnam
Parking: Car park in Dunkeld and Birnam
Picnic Site: Jubilee Park, Birnam
Toilet Facilities: In Birnam
Information Leaflet: Available at Dunkeld Tourist Information Centre.

On the approach to Birnam, either on the A9 from Perth or on the Highland railway, the visitor first encounters the beauty of Highland scenery, with shapely wooded hills on all sides.

Birnam Hill, rising steeply to 1300ft, is the last outpost of the Grampian Mountains along the Tay Valley, and as such gives fine views: not only westwards, back into the hills of Perthshire, but also to the south and east, across the fertile plains of central Scotland.

* You can park at the new car park just out of Birnam at the railway underpass to Birnam Quarry up the Bankfoot B867 road. From here, proceed under the arch and follow the path up the hill to your left, this joins an estate track; go right and carry on up the track. At the junction of these two tracks a short detour can be enjoyed by turning sharp left to King's Rock, or right to Rohallion Castle.

Returning to the original track carry on up to Stair Bridge. The views from this point are splendid, taking in Robin's Dam, Rohallion Lodge and the River Tay going down to Perth.

Return to the main track from Stair Bridge, proceed up the hill to the right, follow the path taking a right along the foot of the cliff to the steps. The steps lead up to the summit, known as the Kings Seat.

Leaving the summit in the opposite direction, follow a narrow path through the heather northwards to a rocky outcrop, set in a stand of Scots pine at around 100ft. The views from this point are extensive including Birnam, Dunkeld and towards Loch of the Lowes.

Walk carefully down the very steep path ahead of you and return either along the foot of the hill to Birnam Quarry car park or out under the A9 to Birnam town centre.

* To lengthen the walk there are two alternative starting points: park in Birnam itself, go up the road opposite the Birnam Hotel under the railway bridges, turn slightly to the right at the houses above the railway, take the path up the hill; this is extremely steep. Alternatively turn left at the houses, follow the lane along the foot of the hill parallel to the railway and join the beginning of the walk.

This walk forms part of the much larger, fully waymarked Dunkeld and Birnam Walks System (see also Walks 26 & 29 in this book).

Pine – pairs of needles from single stalk.

28 Dunkeld Heritage Trail

Grid Ref: 026 429 (car park) **Map Sheets:** 52 or 53

A short walk encompassing places of historical and architectural interest in and around the ancient town of Dunkeld

Length: 2 miles
Height Climbed: Negligible
Grade: C
Public Transport: Regular bus and train services to and from Dunkeld
Parking: Car park at north end of Atholl Street
Picnic Site: On trail in Stanley Park (by Stanley Hill)
Toilet Facilities: The Cross; Atholl Street car park
Information Leaflet and Guide Book Available at Dunkeld Tourist Information Centre.

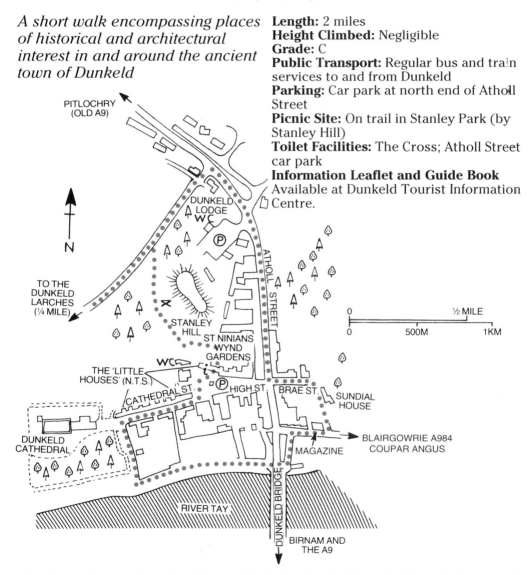

Few places have played as large a part in the history of Scotland as has the small whitewashed town of Dunkeld, situated on the banks of the River Tay.

It first rose to prominence as a stronghold of the Picts in pre-Christian times, and received a further boost when it was proclaimed the ecclesiastical capital of Scotland by the country's first king, Kenneth McAlpin, in the year 850. This religious importance was consolidated in 1318 when work began on Dunkeld Cathedral. The building was completed over a period of two centuries, only to be reduced to a ruin by local lairds in 1560, at the height of the Reformation. The choir was restored, and now serves as the parish church, but the rest of the building remains without a roof. It is now a haven of peace, close by the banks of the Tay.

Dunkeld has been called the 'Gateway to the Highlands', and indeed the Tay Valley is still the most important road and rail route into the region. However, Dunkeld's position - straddling the 'Highland Line'; the southern boundary of the Grampian Mountains - was of far greater importance in the days when it was one of the favoured meeting places of the conflicting Highland and Lowland cultures. This position gave Dunkeld its importance as a trading centre, but the friction of cultures also proved its downfall when it was burnt to the ground by the Cameronians - fighting for William of Orange - in 1689, in order to flush out an invading Highland army which supported James VII.

Little survived the fire, but this walk, which starts beside the Visitor Centre in the High Street, is a tour of the new town which was built to replace it, and it passes by many places and objects of interest, including the oddly shaped Stanley Hill, which was possibly the site of the original dun (or fort) which gave Dunkeld its name. Also on the route are the Dunkeld Larches, including one of the earliest specimens of this tree to be planted in Scotland, which was brought from the Tyrol in a portmanteau and planted in 1738. The descendants of these trees include the Dunkeld Hybrid Larch, which is now widely used in forestry.

Among the other points of interest on this route are Dunkeld Bridge (designed by Telford and opened in 1801); the cathedral; and the 'Little Houses', a row of buildings lining Cathedral Street which have been restored by the National Trust for Scotland.

Further information on this trail, and on the town of Dunkeld, can be found in a leaflet, available from the Visitor Centre, and in a more detailed colour guidebook.

Dunkeld Cathedral

29 *Hermitage and River Braan*

Grid Ref: 012 422 (car park) **Map Sheet:** 52 or 53

A series of good paths centred on a short nature trail, including various types of woodland, plus water falls and romantic follies, forming part of the fully waymarked Dunkeld and Birnam Walks System.

Length: 1 mile – 3½
Height Climbed: 150ft/45m
Grade: C
Public Transport: Regular bus and train services to and from Dunkeld and Birnam
Parking: Hermitage car park (off the A9), also at Rumbling Bridge and near Iver
Picnic Site: In car park
Toilet Facilities: In Dunkeld
Information Leaflet: Available from Dunkeld Tourist Information Centre.

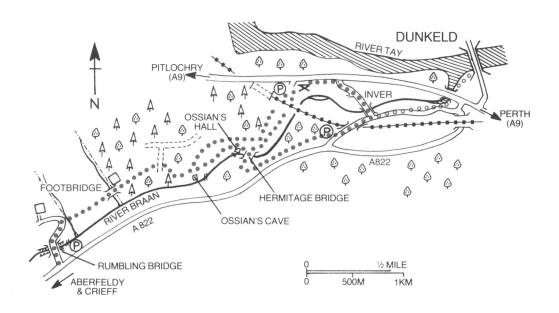

The centrepieces of this pleasant woodland walk, maintained by the National Trust for Scotland, are the River Braan, which breaks into a number of waterfalls and rapids along the route; and two romantically situated 18th century follies, dedicated to the semi-mythical poet Ossian, who is supposed to have lived and written his heroic verse around the 3rd century.

To reach the walk, drive one mile north of Dunkeld on the A9, and follow the signposts to the car park on the left hand side of the road. Here it is possible to obtain a booklet - in return for a small donation - from a dispenser in the car park, which provides a commentary for a nature trail along the route.

Follow the path under the railway line, and on up the river bank until you reach Ossian's Hall. This folly - built on a rocky outcrop overlooking the turbulent Black Linn Fall - was built for the 2nd Duke of Atholl in 1758, in an area already set aside for exotic trees. Unfortunately, the fruit trees and flowering shrubs have now vanished, as have the mirrors which used to line the inside of the building in order to reflect the waterfall, but you still get a fine view - especially when the river is in spate - and a large cedar of Lebanon still stands near the building. Apart from this tree, the mixed woodland also contains a number of large pine and fir trees (including a Douglas fir which is reputed to be the tallest tree in Britain) and a wide variety of deciduous trees.

From the hall, continue up the bank to Ossian's Cave, which is not so much a cave in fact as a group of large rocks with a cleverly constructed stone roof, built to represent a hermit's shelter.

From here the nature trail turns hard right and doubles back through the wood to the car park. Alternatively, you may wish to continue up the river. If so, follow the path (which veers to the right) until you reach a crossroads; walk straight across the larger track and follow the path opposite. This continues through the woods, over a footbridge, across a field and (turning left) down a metalled road to Rumbling Bridge, a small one span bridge over a cleft in the rock through which the river surges with impressive power.

Another alternative route is to return to Ossian's Hall, cross the bridge beside it, and follow the path before you to a small car park and a metalled road; turn left down the hill and cross the bridge into the village of Inver, the birthplace of Niel Gow the fiddler. Continue along the road through the village, turn left along the A9 for about 100yds, and you are back at the car park where you started.

Ossian's Hall – The Hermitage

30 Bishop Hill

Grid Ref: 185 017 (north end of Scotlandwell) **Map Sheet:** 58

A short steep walk up the side of the Lomond Hills, giving excellent views, particularly of Loch Leven and the Ochil Hills beyond.

Length: 4 miles (there and back)
Height Climbed: 1100ft/340m
Grade: B
Public Transport: Bus service to Scotlandwell from Kinross or Milnathort
Parking: by the road side at the start
Toilet Facilities: Kinross

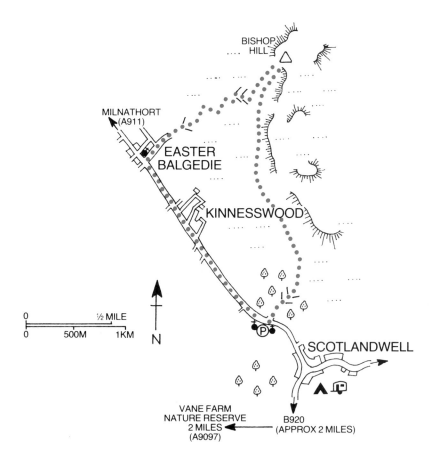

The shallow Loch Leven and its surrounding farmland lie in a natural amphitheatre, with the Ochil Hills, the Cleish Hills, Benarty Hill, Bishop Hill and the Lomonds providing an uneven screen around the small, flat plain which comprised the old County of Kinross. Of all these hills, the range of the Lomonds and Bishop Hill are perhaps the best-remembered landmark, with their abrupt western edge rising from the farmland to the east of Loch Leven to a height of 1700ft/522m (West Lomond) in one grand sweep.

To reach the walk from Kinross, leave the town on the A922, and turn onto the A911 at Milnathort. The walk starts at Scotlandwell - about six miles from Kinross, at the junction of the A911 and the B920. Parking is a little difficult in the village itself, but there is a car park by the church at the start of the walk.

The path to Bishop Hill (1500ft/460m) is signposted, leading up the hill from the north end of Scotlandwell, steeply at first, before running along the face of the hills for about a mile to the summit. It is not necessary to keep to the path if you don't wish to however. The tops of these hills are easy walking terrain - open, springy grassland, spread across an assortment of rounded peaks and hillocks - and it can be an enchanting place, especially on a clear day, when the views are magnificent: east into Fife; south, across the Firth of Forth, to Edinburgh and Lothian; north to the Ochils and the Grampians beyond; and west across Loch Leven to Kinross. From here you have a fine view of Castle Island on the loch below, where Mary Queen of Scots was imprisoned in 1567-8.

The hills are made up of a variety of rocks, both sedimentary and volcanic, the latter giving them their impressive shape. Limestone, a sedimentary rock, was quarried at the summit of Bishop Hill and simply dropped down its steep western slope.

You can leave the hills either at Easter Balgedie, immediately below Bishop Hill, and 2 miles from where you started the walk, or you can return to Scotlandwell by the route you came. The village takes its name from a spring which bubbles up into a 19th century cistern, and which was once highly esteemed as a curative.

Both Kinnesswood and Scotlandwell have a number of very well maintained traditional cottages, and the birthplace of Michael Bruce the Poet may be visited in Kinnesswood (keys from Buchan's Garage).

If you wish an alternative way back to Kinross, take the B920 road, and turn right onto the B9097 when you reach the junction. On the way around the south side of Loch Leven you will pass the Vane Farm Nature Reserve, which is particularly handy for watching the large numbers of waterfowl, particularly geese, which inhabit the loch at various times of the year.

Turn right onto the B996 at the next junction to return to Kinross.

31 *Abernethy Glen*

Grid Ref: 191 164 (Abernethy Round Tower) **Map Sheet:** 58

A short walk along rough tracks in the hills behind Abernethy, with a possible extension to climb Castle Law, with its ruined fort and splendid views over the Tay Estuary.

Length: 2 miles
Height Climbed: 600ft/180m
Grade: B/C – waterproof footwear advisable
Public Transport: Bus service from Perth
Parking: In Abernethy

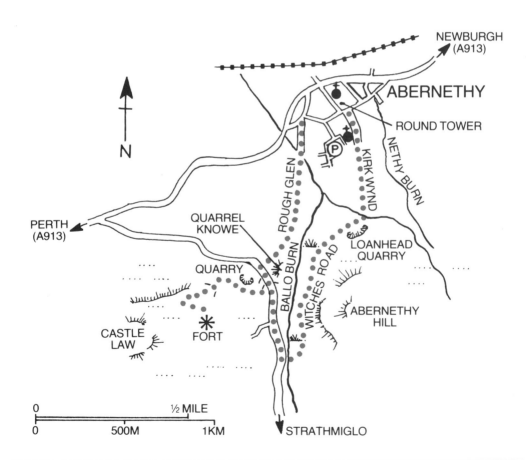

Abernethy, situated on the fertile plain between the Ochil Hills and the Tay Estuary, is a very old settlement, and has strong historical associations, not only with the Picts (the name 'Abernethy' is taken from a certain King Nechtan) and the Romans (there was a legionary fortress at Carpow), but also with the early Church in Scotland.

The town was once the seat of the Bishops of the Pictish kingdom, and later, in the dark ages, it became an important centre for learning. But its most obvious link with the past is the 74ft/23m Abernethy Round Tower - one of only two such towers existing in Scotland - which is believed to have been built in the early 9th century, and to have acted as both a belfry and a place of refuge for the monks who inhabited the nearby monastery. The other Round Tower is at Brechin, 38 miles north-east. Look also for the fragment of a Pictish sculptured stone, placed at the foot of the tower, which dates from around two centuries earlier.

This walk up Abernethy Glen takes you from the edge of the town up into the foothills of the Ochils, and gives you an idea both of the beauty of this corner of Perthshire, and of its historical interest. The centre of Abernethy, with its typically Scottish 18th and 19th century cottages, is a conservation area.

Start from the Tower, turn left out of the village square, then right and up Kirk Wynd to Loanhead Quarry. From here, the path bends right and leads around the face of the hill and into the valley of the Ballo Burn. At this point the path is called the Witches Road, in memory of the members of a local coven, who were ultimately captured, burned, and had their ashes scattered on Abernethy Hill, to your left. There are seats from which you can enjoy the view across the lower Earn Valley.

The path now drops down to cross the Ballo Burn, and joins the road between Glenfoot and Strathmiglo. Turn right and follow the road until you see a sign and a path leading up the Castle Law to your left. This is quite a steep climb in places. At the summit of the hill there are the remains of an Iron Age fort, and from this point you will get fine views of Strathearn, the Grampians, the Braes of the Carse and the Firth of Tay.

Return to the road by the same route, and turn left. Just after Quarrel Knowe (a hill to your right which was once used for archery practice) turn right, into a lay-by. From here a path called the Rough Glen, once part of the old public road and still covered in places with the original stone paving, returns you to the west end of Abernethy.

You should note that the ground around the Ballo Burn can be very marshy, and after rain the Rough Glen tends to live up to its name, so be sure to wear waterproof footwear.

32 *Bonhard Circular Walk*

Grid Ref: 135 257 (foot of the Den of Scone) **Map Sheet:** 53 or 58

A relaxed tour of the farmland to the north of Perth – typical of the low-lying eastern end of Perthshire – culminating in fine views from Murrayshall Hill.

Length: 6 miles
Height Climbed: 700ft/230m
Grade: B
Public Transport: Regular bus service through New Scone to and from Perth
Parking: New Scone
Toilet Facilities: New Scone

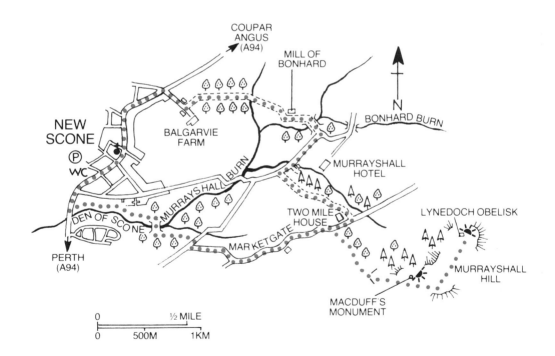

The district of Scone is of great historic interest. Originally it was the site of a Pictish capital, and after becoming the first ruler of both the Picts and the Scots (ie the first King of Scotland) in AD 843, Kenneth MacAlpine brought the Stone of Destiny - an important religious relic - from the west coast to Scone. Here, it was used as the Coronation Stone for the Kings of Scotland, until it was stolen by Edward I of England, in 1296, and became a part of the Coronation Chair in Westminster Abbey.

The village of New Scone was only founded in 1805, when the then Earl of Mansfield decided to move the original village (one mile to the west) a little further from the new palace he was building. It has become a popular and attractive residential settlement, close to but separate from the city of Perth, with several pleasant walks through the surrounding woods and farmland.

This walk leads out of New Scone, and makes a loop through some of the fine farmland to the east of the village, and up the slopes of the Sidlaw Hills, before returning through the Den of Scone. Walk to the north end of the village along the A94, and turn right, opposite Highfield Road, along the track to Balgarvie Farm. When you reach the farm cottages turn left along a side track, and follow this track down a fine avenue of ash trees to the ruined Mill of Bonhard, by the wooded glen of the Bonhard Burn. Turn left along the burn side, cross the burn, and then turn right along the metalled road before you.

Stay on this road until you are beyond the Murrayshall Hotel, and then turn left (beyond the line of trees) up a path to Twomile House. Turn right here, along the metalled road which follows the route of the Marketgate - a medieval road from Perth to Dundee. Stay on this road for a short distance and then turn left (beyond a line of trees marking a field boundary) up Murrayshall Hill, one of the most southerly hills in the Sidlaw range. At the top of the hill there is a romantic folly known as McDuff's Monument, and an obelisk, erected in memory of Thomas Graham of Balgown, the first Lord Lynedoch, who is best remembered for his victory over the French at Barrosa in 1811. Return to the Marketgate by the same route and turn left.

After about one mile the road reaches a junction. Turn right here, and then left again through a gate into the woodland around the Den of Scone, a deep narrow glen holding the Murrayshall Burn. The path beside the burn leads you back to Scone.

This walk may easily be combined with a visit to Scone Palace and grounds, just over a mile to the west, reached from the top of the village by turning off the A94 along Stormont Road.

33 Kinnoull Hill Woodland Park (East)

Grid Ref: 145 236 (Jubilee Car Park) **Map Sheet:** 58 or 53

Two short walks through coniferous woodland giving views over the Tay Valley and the neighbouring hills.

Length: 1½ miles and 2½ miles
Height Climbed: Undulating
Grade: C
Public Transport: Bus to the bottom of Kinnoull Hill
Parking: Jubilee car park
Toilet Facilities: Opposite car park
Information Leaflet available from Perth Tourist Information Centre

PERTH (1 MILE)

PERTH

CORSIEHILL

WC

P   FORT

DEUCHNY WOOD

DEUCHNY HILL

CONTINUATION ROUTE 34

DEUCHNY BURN

KINNOULL HILL

KINNOULL TOWER

WINDY GHOULL

KINFAUNS CASTLE

KINFAUNS AND GLEN CARSE

EDINBURGH (M90)

PERTH

RIVER TAY

DUNDEE (A90)

N

0   ½ MILE
0   500M   1KM

Two miles from the centre of Perth, on a small road which passes to the north of Kinnoull Hill before dropping into the Carse of Gowrie, there is a car park - situated in the pass between Kinnoull Hill and Deuchny Hill. From this central position it is possible to take two separate routes - one on each of the hills - neither of which taxes the walker greatly, and both of which give splendid views of the Tay Valley and the surrounding countryside. On a clear day the vista is outstanding, embracing the long line of hills from Ben Vorlich beyond Strathearn in the west, to the mountains of Angus northwards across Strathmore.

To follow the Kinnoull Hill route (the shorter of the two), cross the road, and follow the indicator for Tower Walk along the edge of the thick woodland. From here there are fine views across the Deuchny Burn to Kinfauns Castle (built in 1825 for the Earl of Moray and now a centre for walking holidays) and the River Tay beyond. From here the path leads on along the steep cliffs of Kinnoull Hill to Kinnoull Tower, with the deep gully of Windy Ghoull - famous for its echoes - beyond it. The tower, and another on a hill just to the north-east, were built as ruins by the 9th Earl of Kinnoull and his neighbour in the 18th century, in imitation of the castles they had seen along the Rhine Valley. From the tower you have excellent views of the Carse of Gowrie, and of the Ochil Hills and Fife on the far side of the valley, but don't venture too close to the cliff edge!

From the Tower, follow the directions for the Nature Walk and then the signs showing the way to the Jubilee car park. If visiting the summit follow the signs for Tower Walk down Kinnoull Hill at the back of Corsiehill which leads to the Jubilee car park.

The route around Deuchny Hill is a little longer, but the path is generally good and every bit as interesting. Leave the car park by the main entrance and turn right up a well-marked track, leaving the wood to your right. After a short way the track enters the wood, but before doing so it is worth enjoying the view: across Perth, back up the Tay Valley and into the Grampians.

The route now travels through dense coniferous forestry, but it is worth visiting the site of an Iron Age fort - on the hill to your right - although only grassy humps remain to show where the walls once were.

The path then turns hard right, to skirt the edge of Deuchny Hill, before cutting left again and returning to the car park.

For further information, collect a copy of the "Kinnoull Hill Woodland Park Forest Walks" leaflet available from Perth Tourist Information Centre.

34 Kinnoull Hill Woodland Park (West)

Grid Ref: 121 234 (Queen's Bridge) Map **Sheet:** 58 or 53

A steep walk; starting from the centre of Perth and rising, through open woodland, to the summit of Kinnoull Hill. Overlooks steep cliffs and gives excellent views, particularly of the Tay Valley and Estuary.

Length: 4 miles
Height Climbed: 700ft/212m
Grade: B
Public Transport: Regular bus and train services to and from Perth
Parking: In Perth, or at Corsiehill
Picnic Sites: On Corsiehill
Toilet Facilities: Perth (South Inch)
Information Leaflet available from Perth Tourist Information Centre

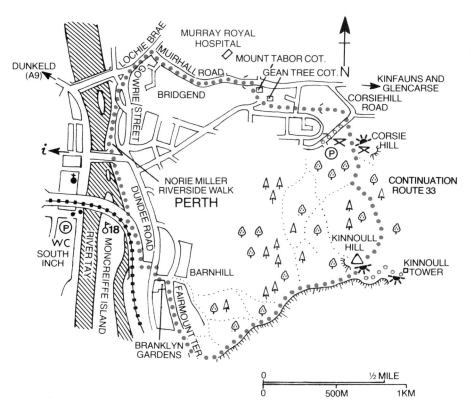

The steep cliffs of Kinnoull Hill, overhanging the Tay Valley to the east of Perth, and crowned by Kinnoull Tower (a romantic folly) are amongst the most dramatic and distinctive landmarks in Perthshire. Since the hill was gifted to the city in 1924, there has been easy access to the extensive walks and views which the area affords. This route takes you from the centre of Perth, up the relatively gentle northern slopes of the hill, and returns along the edge of the spectacular cliffs to the south, which have a sheer drop of 200ft/60m in places.

Starting from the eastern end of the Queen's Bridge, turn left (north) and walk along the Norie Miller riverside walk, which is a landscaped section of the river bank. When you reach the end of this path, at a modern residential development, climb the flight of steps in the wall to your right, cross Gowrie Street and walk up Back Wynd and Lochie Brae, with which it merges.

Turn sharp right, off Lochie Brae, up Muirhall Road (which is flanked to the left by the Murray Royal Hospital), and continue on this road until you reach Mount Tabor Cottage, to your right. Follow the path to the right of the cottage, and turn left at Gean Tree Cottage. Continue straight along the path before you, until you reach Corsie Hill Road, at the edge of the housing. Veer to the right across this road and follow the path ahead up Corsie Hill, where there is a view indicator and some picnic tables.

The car park at Corsiehill is ideal for those who only wish to climb the top section of the hill, or simply enjoy the view without effort!

From the view indicator, follow the path that leads up beyond the quarry, and through woodland to a crossing of paths. Here the route to the summit is signposted to your left and you will soon reach the summit giving a panoramic view over Perth, the Tay Valley, and the Highland Line. Just beyond is the Earl of Kinnoull's Table: a supported stone slab once used by the 9th Earl for picnics. It is important to be careful at this point of the walk, as the cliff drops very suddenly a few yards beyond the table. The views, however, are magnificent, with the Carse of Gowrie to your left (on the Kinnoull side of the River Tay) and Moncrieffe Hill and the Ochil Hills on the far side of the valley.

From here, you can make a brief detour along the cliff-edge to your left, to Kinnoull Tower (see Route 33).

Turning right from the stone table, follow the red waymarkers in reverse, past the picnic site, to signs for Barnhill. Walk to the ruins and follow the sign for Branklyn Garden (famous for its collection of rare alpine plants and primulas) and right, along Dundee road. Turn sharp left, shortly afterwards cross the road and walk down the steps towards Moncreiffe Island. Turn right at the railway bridge to return to the town or cross the Tay by the footpath on the railway bridge.

For further information, collect a copy of the "Kinnoull Hill Woodland Park Forest Walks" leaflet available from Perth Tourist Information Centre.

35 *Old Perth Trail*

Grid Ref: 119 236 (St John's Kirk) **Map Sheet:** 53 or 58

These two walks lead you through Perth's historical and architectural areas beginning appropriately at the Tourist Information Centre.

Length: 3 walks of approx. 1 mile each
Height Climbed: Negligible
Grade: C
Public Transport: Regular bus and train services to and from Perth
Parking: North Inch; Tay Street; South Inch etc
Toilet Facilities: South Inch
Information Leaflet available from Tourist Information Centre

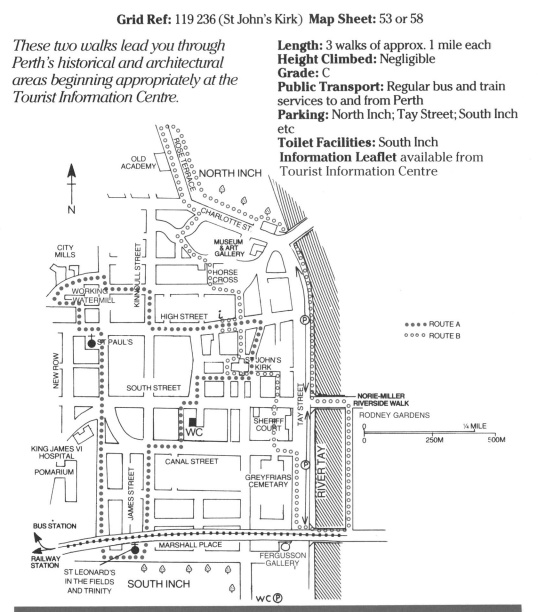

Perth has always owed its prosperity to its position: at first as a natural crossing point for the River Tay, later as a port trading with Europe (although 30 miles from the coast, Perth still has a harbour, placed at the highest navigable point on the Tay Estuary) and latterly as the service centre for the prosperous farming community of eastern Perthshire. Perth is still a working town, with whisky companies, cleaning and glassware manufacturing, and insurance, but the atmosphere is more that of a large country town than that of an industrial centre, and people come from all over the world to see the famous bull sales in spring and autumn. The two walks shown on the map opposite will guide you through the town's historic centre. Look out along the way for display boards and wall plaques describing the buildings and events which helped shape Perth's past.

It is thought that the town may have originated as a Roman fort, but it makes no appearance in the records until the 12th century, when it was already well established. During the medieval period it gradually grew in importance as a centre of government, and was often the seat of the peripatetic Scottish monarchy (James I was murdered in Perth in 1437). During the Reformation, in 1559, John Knox and other religious reformers whipped a crowd of supporters into such a passion that they sacked St John's Kirk (the city's principal church, now restored to its full glory) and a number of nearby monastries.

In 1600, Perth was the scene for the Gowrie Conspiracy, a confrontation between King James VI and John Ruthven (the Earl of Gowrie) and his brother, Alexander. The exact details of the event are a mystery, but the two brothers - who the king claimed had attempted to murder him - were killed, and James was rid of two powerful opponents at one stroke. Among the buildings remaining from this early period is the King James VI Hospital, founded in 1587 and recently restored.

In later years, Perth was involved in both of the Jacobite uprisings of the 18th century (Charles Edward Stuart stayed at the Salutation Hotel in South Street, and drilled his army on the North Inch), while in later years the town settled down to a more peaceful and prosperous existence, with fine terraces of Georgian town houses being built facing across the North and South Inches - two flat riverside parks at either end of the town, both with play equipment for children.

A leaflet describing the 'Old Perth Trail' along a slightly different route, is available from Perth Tourist Information Centre.

36 *Ben Vrackie*

Grid Ref: 944 597 (car park)   **Map Sheets:** 43 and 52

A hill walk crossing an area of typical Scottish moorland scenery, before rising to a summit with panoramic views.

Length: 6 miles (there and back)
Height Climbed: 2320ft/734m (from Pitlochry)
Grade: A/B
Public Transport: Regular bus and train services to and from Pitlochry
Parking: Small car park at start of walk, otherwise anywhere in Pitlochry
Toilet Facilities: In Pitlochry

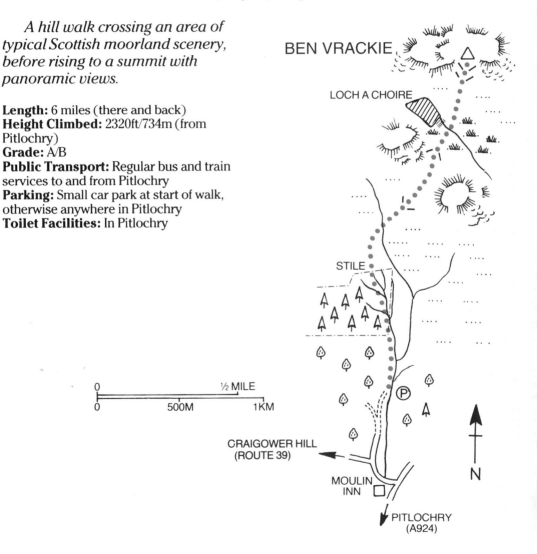

BEN VRACKIE

LOCH A CHOIRE

STILE

0   ½ MILE
0   500M   1KM

CRAIGOWER HILL
(ROUTE 39)

MOULIN
INN

PITLOCHRY
(A924)

N

Ben Vrackie rises above Pitlochry to the height of 2757ft, and gives not only excellent views of the surrounding mountains, but also a very pleasant walk through some typical Scottish moorland scenery.

The walk can be started from either Pitlochry or Moulin, but it is worth remembering that the car park at Moulin is very small, and on busy days it would be wiser to leave your vehicle in Pitlochry if possible. Starting from Pitlochry, follow the A924 road to Moulin (a distance of under a mile), and turn left at the Moulin Inn. The road here is signposted for the walk. Follow the road until the small car park is reached amongst the trees on your right hand side. The path is clearly marked here through the trees lining a small burn, until it reaches a deer fence at the edge of the moor over which there is a stile.

The path then rises gently through the heather, and passes between two small hills, before descending again, and crossing some very marshy ground below Loch a' Choire. You are now below the final slope. Follow the badly-eroded path to the summit, leaving the broken rocks and scree to your left until you reach the ridge, and then turn left for the peak. Return by the same route.

The path on this walk is generally well trodden and the going is relatively easy, if a little damp in places, and steep in the final ascent. Along the route you cross some truly bleak landscape without leaving civilisation too far behind, and you should see at least one of the financial assets of the area, the Red Grouse, which is common here. Watch also for Red Deer along the hillsides.

On the summit there is a horizontal dial, which indicates those hills which are visible from that point, including Schiehallion, Ben Lawers, the Cairngorms and Arthurs Seat in Edinburgh.

As with all hill climbs, try to pick a clear day for your walk, as low cloud will obliterate your view. In spite of the accessibility of the mountain from Pitlochry, the safety precautions and equipment required for mountain walks (see introduction) are just as essential as on more isolated hills, and weather conditions can change just as quickly.

Red Deer Stag

37 *The Black Spout and Donavourd*

Grid Ref: 952 575 (Black Spout car park) **Map Sheet:** 52 or 53

A short walk through woodland and open farmland past a delightful waterfall.

Length: 2-3 miles
Height Climbed: Negligible
Grade: C
Public Transport: Regular bus and train services to and from Pitlochry
Parking: In Pitlochry and Black Spout Wood
Picnic Sites: Benches on route
Toilet Facilities: In Pitlochry

'Black Spout' is a waterfall, pleasantly situated in a small gorge on the Edradour burn. The path leading to it can be rather confusing, but it passes through some charming countryside of fields and open woodland, and there is no real danger of becoming lost. This walk has the added advantage, for anyone staying in Pitlochry, of not requiring any driving.

From the East Moulin road, start along Tomcroy Terrace. When this road ends turn right, and, after a few yards, a gate will open on to a field on your left. Walk to the gate on the opposite side of this field, and follow the path which then descends to a bridge across the tree-lined Kinnaird burn; then turn right, through another gate and into another field. The path becomes a little indistinct here, but you should head towards the wood diagonally across the field before you, where there is a style over the boundary fence. After this the route becomes more obvious again. Follow the path through the wood, across the dirt road, and onwards, keeping the cottages to your left. There you will find a signpost to the Black Spout, and if you continue on the path you will reach an exciting viewing platform which projects out above the falls.

From here there are two options. You can turn left again up the burn, cross the bridge and follow the path through the farm buildings ahead to join an unnumbered road at Milton of Edradour and the Edradour Distillery which is open and well worth visiting. You can then turn right, past Donavourd, to join the old A9, and turn right again to reach Pitlochry (it should be noted that this road can be very busy and would not be suitable for animals or small children). Alternatively, cut right from the viewing platform at the fall (ignoring the path down the burn) and carry on until you reach the dirt road. Follow this for about 300 yards before striking off left, following the signpost to Pitlochry. This leads to another footbridge over the Kinnaird burn, just below the Atholl Palace Hotel; turn left after the bridge and keep on until you reach Knockfarrie Road. This will take you back towards the town centre.

The Black Spout falls in total around 150 feet, and is a romantic spot. The route to and from it, through a variety of mixed woodland, is well endowed with places of beauty and other paths. A number of benches are provided which are useful for picnics.

There is also now a car park gained from an access road off the Perth road, under the railway at the bottom south-east corner of the woodland. A short walk from here along the Perth road takes you to the Blair Atholl Distillery, another attraction which is well worth a visit.

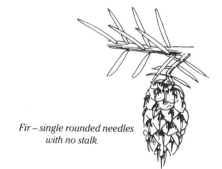

Fir – single rounded needles with no stalk.

38 *Corrour to Rannoch Station*

Grid Ref: 423 578 (Rannoch Station) **Map Sheets:** 41 and 51

A train journey to Corrour from Rannoch Station, with a long hike to return, across rough, open moorland.

Length: 9 miles
Height Climbed: 330ft/100m
Grade: A
Public Transport: Mail bus to and from Rannoch Station from Kinloch Rannoch; Rail service to and from Glasgow and Fort William
Parking: Rannoch Station
Toilet Facilities: Rannoch Station

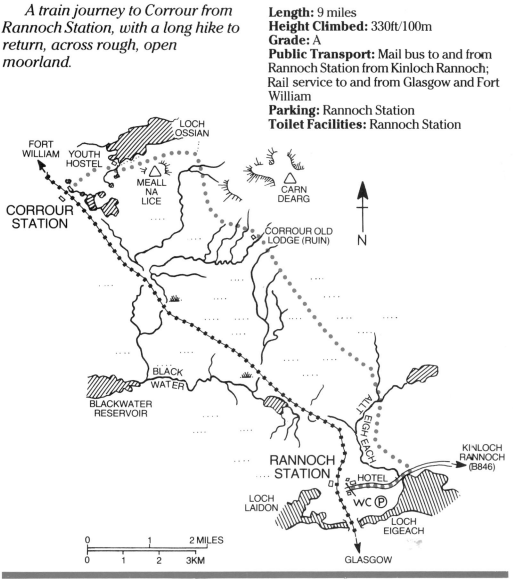

Rannoch Moor is a bleak but fascinating place. During the ice-age it acted as a vast reservoir of glacial ice, originating in the surrounding hills, which was then forced down the valleys of the River Tummel, Loch Ericht, Glen Etive etc, which radiate from the moor. Subsequently it was covered in thick pine forest, the remnants of which can still be seen in the Black Wood of Rannoch. But only old stumps, preserved on the peat, now remain on the moor - embedded beneath the wide blanket-bog which the area has become, crossed only by the West Highland railway line.

To reach the moor, drive west along Loch Tummel on the B8019 to Tummel Bridge, and then continue along Loch Rannoch on the B846 to Rannoch Station. Leave your car here and take the train to Corrour (be sure to check the train times before setting off, and leave plenty of time to reach the station, as the roads are narrow). The train journey takes from 10 to 15 minutes, passing through the characteristic landscape of small, heath covered mounds, surrounded by burns, lochans, bogs and peat hags. The unstable peat is so deep in places that the railway line has to be supported by 'floating' it on bundles of brushwood.

Once at your destination (there is no road to Corrour, and only one house), walk eastwards on the track to the Youth Hostel at the southern end of Loch Ossian - a place of great beauty, set in a ring of high peaks. Continue, past the Hostel, and along a track to the east of Loch Ossian (not the track nearest the water's edge, but the one above it), which veers away from the loch, and cuts east; between the craggy stump of Meall na Lice (1906ft/583m) to the right, and the massive rounded bulk of Carn Dearg (3080ft/939m) to the left, along whose flank the easily followed path now runs.

About 3 miles from the Youth Hostel, you pass the ruin of Corrour Old Lodge. At this point the railway runs across the moor below you to the right. Beyond the moor is the Blackwater Reservoir, and beyond the Reservoir are the mountains around Glencoe, with Ben Nevis and its attendant peaks to the north of them.

Continue along the path, crossing Allt Eigeach, and rejoining the B846 to Rannoch Station where the road passes Loch Eigeach. Turn right along this road for 1¼ miles to regain the station. The local hotel is close at hand, to provide welcome refreshment and relaxation at the end of the walk.

39 *Craigower Hill*

Grid Ref: 944 593 (Rannoch Station) **Map Sheets:** 43 and 52

A steep climb along good paths, through a Forestry Commission plantation, to a noted local viewpoint.

Length: 3 miles (round trip)
Height Climbed: 810ft/248m
Grade: B
Public Transport: Regular bus and train services to and from Pitlochry
Parking: In Pitlochry
Toilet Facilities: In Pitlochry
Information leaflet available (National Trust for Scotland)

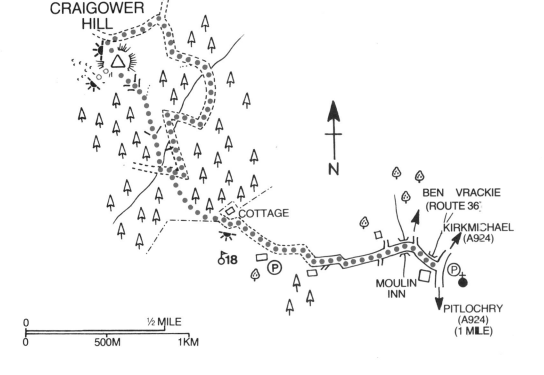

90

Craigower is an old beacon hill, a rocky outcrop jutting out above Pitlochry. It is not particularly high (1300ft/450m), but its position above the confluence of the Tummel and Garry rivers gives it splendid views up both valleys, and also down the Tummel and Tay towards Dunkeld.

From Pitlochry, follow the A924 as far as Moulin, and then turn left behind the Moulin Hotel, a fine old coaching inn. Continue along this road, following the signs for Craigower, until you reach the golf course. The road here crosses the course, so be sure that no one is playing before you cross. On the other side of the course the path passes in front of a small cottage, before striking up through the coniferous woods which cover the slopes of Craigower. The route through the wood is well signposted and should present no difficulties, though it does become rather steep as you near the summit of the hill.

The trees have been cleared from the top, and an annotated photograph placed atop a plinth explains the westward view which includes Loch Tummel, Loch Rannoch, Farragon Hill, Schiehallion and Glencoe beyond. Unfortunately there is no similar facility to explain the eastward view, but there is a bench where you can relax and enjoy it.

It is worthwhile descending a little way (with care) south-west from the summit where the view over Pitlochry and Strathtummel becomes even more extensive. Retrace your steps to the summit for the descent.

The summit of the hill was given to the National Trust for Scotland in 1947 by Mrs M.D.Fergusson of Baledmund, in memory of her father.

If you wish to return by a different route, then follow the markers leading west from the summit, and the path will bring you back round the hill, along a Forestry Commission road, to rejoin your original path before you reach the golf course.

No special equipment is required for this walk - although a map would be useful if you wish to decipher the view to the east - but bear in mind that the steep top section of the hill can be very slippery when wet, so that walking boots are advised.

Larch – clusters of needles.

40 *Falls of Bruar*

Grid Ref: 823 611 (car park) **Map Sheet:** 43

A romantic walk on well-maintained paths along a short but spectacular river gorge, with fine waterfalls.

Length: 1½ miles
Height Climbed: 400ft/120m
Grade: C
Public Transport: None
Parking: Car park at foot of walk
Picnic Sites: On walk and beside Hotel
Toilet Facilities: Bruar car park (April-October)
Information Leaflet available from cairn at foot of walk

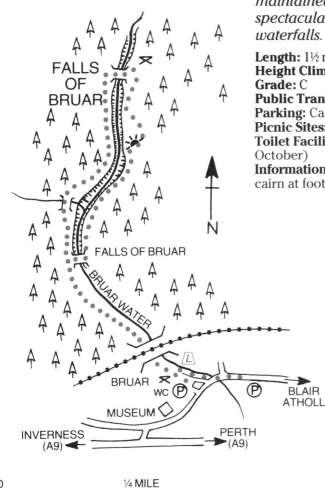

Bruar is a small group of houses some eight miles north-west of Pitlochry, just off the A9 to Inverness. Its most remarkable feature is that, in the Baluain Wood which clothes the hill behind it, there is a particularly beautiful river gorge, celebrated in poetry by Robert Burns in 1781:

'Here, foaming down the shelvy rocks,
    In twisting strength I rin;
There, high my boiling torrent smokes,
    Wild roaring o'er the linn'

He went on to complain of a lack of trees along the riverside, but with this flaw now remedied, the spot is surely as picturesque as the poet could ever have wished.

The car park is situated next to the Clan Donnachaidh Museum. This museum tells the history of the Robertsons - at one time a powerful clan in this district - and is well worth visiting while you are in Bruar.

The walk itself, clearly signposted, starts beside the museum, runs up under the railway line, and on through the mixed coniferous woods on the cliff edges which overhang the Bruar Water. Because the river passes over rock here, the water is surprisingly clear, and does not have the brown, peaty colour usually found in highland rivers. This enables you to see more clearly the complex patterns cut into the rock by the fast flowing water.

There are two major falls on the river, both crossed by footbridges, with a small picnic area just above the upper falls. Do not be frustrated if the trees seem, at first, to obscure your view of the upper falls on the return journey; a short way down the east side of the glen there is a viewpoint which gives a splendid prospect of the major element of the falls - a 30ft direct drop - with the stone footbridge balanced above it.

This is a relaxed walk around a truly picturesque spot, and is well worth a visit, but parents of young children are advised to keep their charges under strict control, as in places, the path runs very close to the edge of the steep cliffs above the river. As with other waterfalls, this walk can offer a good alternative to a hillwalk on a wet day, as the local hotel at Cauline is on hand to provide shelter and inner warmth afterwards.

Spruce – single pointed needle on stalk.

41 *Garry – Tummel Walk System*

Grid Ref: 913 610 (Garry Bridge car park) **Map Sheet:** 43 and 52

A system of good paths through varied woodland beside river and loch, including the spectacular pass of Killiecrankie.

Length: 8½ miles
Grade: C
Public Transport: Regular bus and train services to and from Pitlochry
Parking: Pitlochry; Garry Bridge; Loch Dunmore; Faskally; Killiecrankie Information Centre; Clunie Power Station
Picnic Sites: Killiecrankie Information Centre; Loch Dunmore car park; Clunie Power Station
Toilet Facilities: Pitlochry; Killiecrankie Information Centre; Loch Dunmore car park

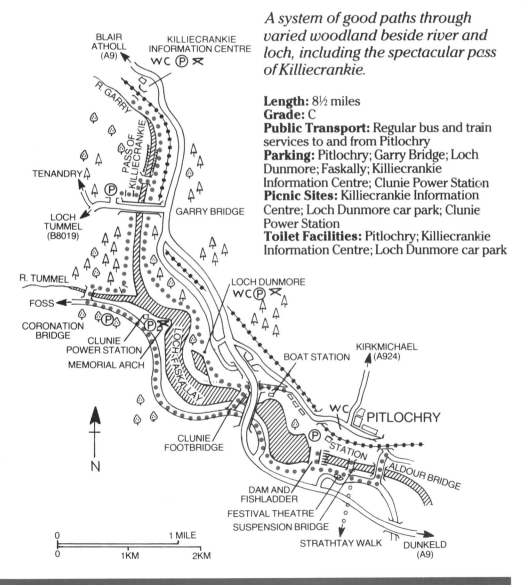

94

There are many footpaths around Pitlochry, with numerous possible variations, as described in the leaflet available at the Tourist Information Centre.

This round walk, taking in Loch Faskally and the Rivers Tummel and Garry, is pleasant at any time of the year, but to be seen at its best it should be walked in September or October when the leaves on the trees are changing. Perthshire is justly famous for its autumn colours, and few areas show the Larch, Birch and Oak off to better effect, in this respect, than that encompassed by this walk.

Starting from Pitlochry, leave the town on the north road, and veer to the left down Clunie Bridge Road just as the houses end. This road leads to a boat station where rowing boats can be hired during the summer season. Continue along the path beyond the boat station, before turning to the right to pass Loch Dunmore (where there is a car park). From here continue along the metalled road which is signposted for Killiecrankie. The road leads you round a bay in the loch, and past the Freshwater Fisheries Laboratory, before directing you sharp left down a small path which leads up the River Garry to the Garry Bridge over the Pass of Killiecrankie, where there is another car park.

From here you can either: continue up the east side of the river, through the picturesque river gorge, to the National Trust Information Centre at Killiecrankie (one mile) which includes information on the Battle of Killiecrankie (1689); or you can cross the river by the footbridge just beyond the road bridge, and turn sharp left to walk downstream once again.

The latter path takes you south along the banks of the River Garry before turning west up the River Tummel. Continue along the side of the river, walking through an extensive Larch wood, and passing close by the rough water of the Linn of Tummel, before crossing it by a small suspension bridge called the Coronation Bridge. This section of the walk is part of a National Trust nature trail, and has indicators along its route.

Turn left once you are over the bridge, and continue along the metalled road down the west side of Loch Faskally, passing by the memorial arch commemorating the opening of the Clunie Power Station. There are four alternative crossing-points to return to Pitlochry: first Clunie Bridge, to the north-west of the town; second, the dam, with its exhibition and fish ladder; third, the suspension bridge leading to the centre of the town, and overlooked by the new Festival Theatre; and finally, Aldour Bridge, to the south-east end of Pitlochry.

This is an easy, well-maintained path, and nothing more specialised than comfortable footwear should be required. Apart from the waterfowl and woodland birdlife, watch particularly for red squirrels along this route.

42 Glen Tilt

Grid Ref: 875 655 (Blair Atholl Caravan Site – start of walk) **Map Sheet:** 43

A long walk, along paths of varying quality, through a typical steep-sided Highland glen, passing through woodland and farmland.

Length: 10½ miles or 6½ miles
Height Climbed 300ft/90m
Grade: B
Public Transport: Bus and train services from Pitlochry
Parking: In Blair Atholl village
Toilet Facilities: In Blair Atholl village
Information Leaflet available from Castle or Caravan Site

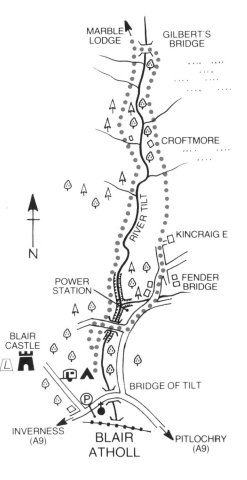

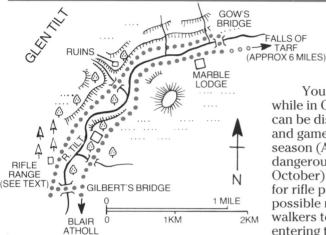

GLEN TILT

GOW'S BRIDGE

RUINS

FALLS OF TARF
(APPROX 6 MILES)

MARBLE LODGE

RIFLE RANGE
(SEE TEXT)

R. TILT

GILBERT'S BRIDGE

N

0   1 MILE
0   1KM   2KM

BLAIR ATHOLL

You are asked to stay on the path while in Glen Tilt, as walking on the hills can be disturbing for both farm animals and game birds, while during the shooting season (August-October) it is potentially dangerous. Also, at the weekend (March-October) the west bank of the river is used for rifle practice, however access is still possible most weekends. It is advisable for walkers to check with the Marshal before entering the area.

If you find yourself tiring while on this walk, remember that the route can be shortened by 4 miles, simply by crossing the river at Gilbert's Bridge and walking downstream from there.

For those who are interested in longer walks, there is a right of way through Glen Tilt and over to the Linn of Dee. There is limited access for vehicles up a private road to reduce the length of this walk, but prior permission must be received from the Atholl Estate Office and a small fee paid for the use of the road.

While in the area it is well worth paying a visit to Blair Castle (entrance from Blair Atholl), the home of the Duke of Atholl and a building of great interest. It contains fine collections of furniture, china, firearms and Jacobite and family relics. Blair Atholl also has a working meal mill which welcomes visitors, a display of local life and folklore at the Old School, and excellent hotels.

Glen Tilt is a long glen, leading some eleven miles from the broad valley of the River Garry at Blair Atholl - seven miles north-west of Pitlochry on the A9 - up into the hills around the Falls of Tarf, where the river divides into a number of tributaries. This walk enables you to spend a day in the serenity of such a glen, and to enjoy the beauty of the hills, woods and waterfalls for which the area is renowned.

Start walking from the Blair Atholl Caravan Site (the entrance is just beyond the road bridge over the River Tilt, coming from Pitlochry), leaving the site by the first of the gates to the riverside footpath, and following it up through the woods by the river. The path is signposted from this point onwards. A good commentary on objects and places of interest along the route - including a ruined crofting settlement and a private hydro-electric generator - can be obtained by buying a small leaflet, available from the caravan site office and from Blair Castle.

43 Rannoch Forest

Grid Ref: 618 572 **Map Sheet:** 51

A walk through coniferous woodland, some of it natural pinewood, passing along the steeply cut glen of the Bogair Burn.

Length: 5 miles
Height Climbed: 500ft/153m
Grade: B
Public Transport: None
Parking: Car park at start of walks
Picnic Sites: At start of walks and by loch side
Toilet Facilities: At car park
Information Leaflet available from Tummel Forest Information Centre at Queen's View.

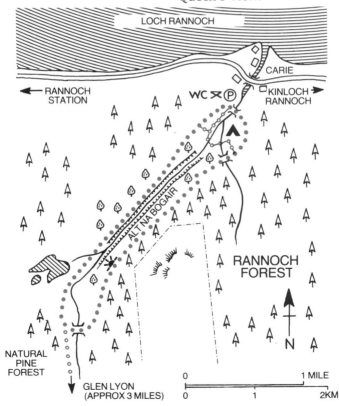

The Black Wood of Rannoch is a peaceful enough place now, but it was not always so. At one time its inhabitants were outlawed and landless clansmen who used the wood as a centre for cattle raids throughout the Scottish Highlands. Indeed, so notorious was the place that to be a man whose 'head is under the wood' became a Gaelic byword for outlawry.

The Black Wood has been much reduced since then by succeeding generations, but its remaining fragments still comprise one of the largest surviving areas of the original Caledonian Pinewoods, which at one time covered the entire Highland area. These fragments are now protected, situated within the larger Forestry Commission plantation of Rannoch Forest.

To find the walks, which are located to the east of the main residual area of the Black Wood, leave Kinloch Rannoch on the road which runs along the south side of Loch Rannoch. Follow this road for around 3 miles. There are two car parks in quick succession on the left hand side of the road; turn into the Carie car park, the second of the two. There is ample space here for parking and picnicking, plus a route map of the signposted paths, two of which are very short and are ideal if you wish simply to stretch your legs. The third and longest walk takes you up the side of Allt na Bogair (Bogair Burn) which flows through a steep-sided gorge.

The gorge contains natural woodland of Scots Pine, Birch and Rowan, while the hills to either side are covered by a man-made forest of Lodgepole Pine, Scots Pine, Sitka Spruce, Larch and Birch. At the furthest extent of the walk, where it crosses the burn to return through the woods on the opposite slope, there is a small stand of naturally seeded Scots Pine, which gives an idea of how the forest would once have looked. Watch also for a wide range of forest birdlife, including capercaillie, blackcock, crossbills and jays.

The walk is a pleasant one, giving good views of Loch Rannoch and the surrounding hills, and it is well signposted and maintained, although patches of mud may be encountered.

For the more adventurous walkers the path can be continued along a right of way to Bridge of Balgie in Glen Lyon, but be sure you don't attempt this route without proper maps and hiking equipment, and consult the estate owners before walking it in the shooting season (August-October).

44 *Strathtay*

Grid Ref: 914 535 (Strathtay end of walk) **Map Sheet:** 52

A gentle hill-walk from Strathtay to the Tummel Valley. The path, vague in places, passes through farmland and coniferous woodland.

Length: 4 miles
Height Climbed: 900ft/275m
Grade: B
Public Transport: Bus service from Pitlochry or Aberfeldy
Parking: Anywhere in Pitlochry; roadsides around Strathtay
Toilet Facilities: In Pitlochry

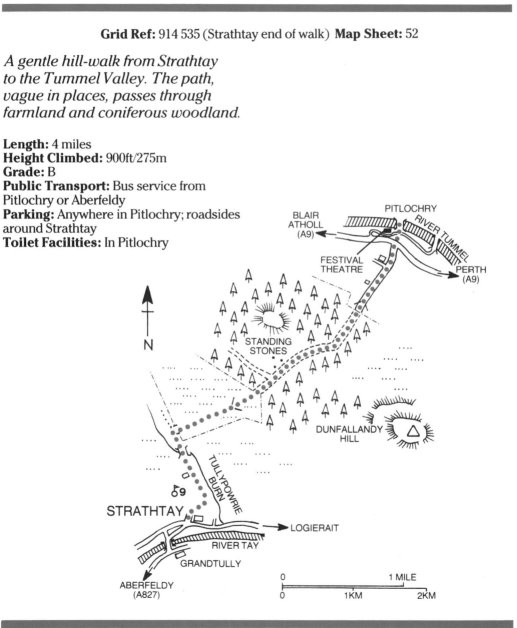

At Logierait the two water systems of the Tummel and the Tay converge. This walk crosses a shoulder of Dunfallandy Hill, which is placed in the V formed by the two rivers, and thus affords fine views of both valleys.

From Pitlochry, take the Aberfeldy bus, and ask to be dropped at Strathtay, just before the road forks to cross the Tay to Grandtully. Here you will find a signpost for the walk to Pitlochry on your right as the bus stops. If you are driving, take the A9 south (from Pitlochry) 3 miles to Ballinluig. Turn onto the A827 to Aberfeldy and follow the signposts for Strathtay.

An alternative, minor road to join the A827 at Logierait runs from Pitlochry on the west side of the River Tummel. This allows a stop-off to see the Dunfallandy Stone, a fine 8th Century Pictish sculptured stone slab a mile south of Pitlochry.

Once on the walk, follow the path around the edge of the golf course, and up the side of the Tullypowrie Burn, which is crossed by a wooden footbridge. Turn right through a gate in a deer fence, and cross the stretch of open moorland before you. The path is rather vague here, but there are posts planted along the route to help you. After about half a mile you enter a forestry plantation, through which your route is well signposted, and a short way into the forest you will find a small group of standing stones in a clearing to your left.

The path then joins a metalled road, which leads you down through open farmland into the Tummel Valley. At one point in the path you must cross the A9; be extremely careful here, and keep any children and animals under strict control.

The walk ends by the Pitlochry Festival Theatre, and from here you can cross the River Tummel to Pitlochry by a small footbridge.

You can of course walk this route in the opposite direction, but be sure that you have checked the times for buses on the return route, or else have arranged alternative transport.

Pitlochry Festival Theatre

45 Tummel Forest

Grid Ref: 864 599 (Queen's View) **Map Sheet:** 43

Three walks of varying lengths on good paths through Forestry Commission plantations, with fine views of Loch Tummel and Schiehallion.

Length: 1½ miles; 2 miles; 3 miles
Height Climbed: 550ft/170m
Grade: B/C
Public Transport: Regular bus service from Pitlochry
Parking: Car park at start of walks
Picnic Sites: Several on walk routes
Toilet Facilities: In car park
Information Leaflet available from Tummel Forest Information Centre at Queen's View.

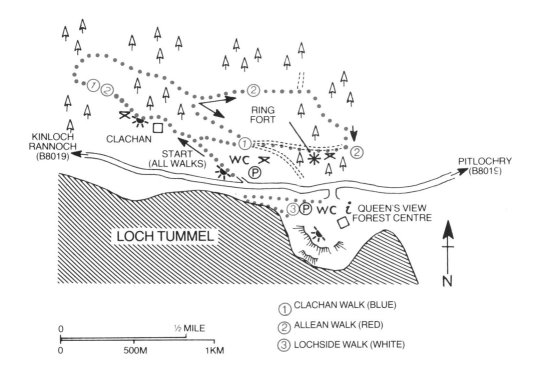

The Forestry Commission have established a number of marked walks through their plantations, which can be found all over the country: they can be relied upon to be well thought out and maintained, and are always popular with lovers of trees and forests.

A fine example of this type of walk can be found in the hills behind the Queen's View, on the north side of Loch Tummel. Follow the B8019 from Pitlochry, north, for about three miles, and then turn left across the Garry Bridge, following the signs for Kinloch Rannoch. Approximately three miles along this road you will find the Queen's View Centre, which is run by the Forestry Commission and supplies information on the forest, its wildlife and walks, as well as the association with Queen Victoria who visited the area in 1866. 300 yards further along the road there are extensive parking facilities for the walks themselves, situated a short distance up a signposted forestry road. There are also toilet facilities and a notice board showing the various routes around the forest.

These routes are well marked, and will lead you past various view points and objects of interest on the way. The times given on the notice board for these walks are rather over-generous and include time for lengthy anticipated stoppages. If a reasonable pace is maintained, each route can be completed in a considerably shorter time than shown - though in such splendid and peaceful surroundings, there is always the temptation to linger.

Two of the three walks pass through the 'clachan', a typical 18th century farm settlement which was discovered while the forest was being planted. The main building has been reconstructed, while the rest of the area is excavated with the remaining buildings being labelled according to their use. Here there is also a spectacular picnic site, on a high rock jutting over the forest with a fine view of Loch Tummel and Schiehallion at its head. There are four other similar sites - all shown on the map - spaced out along the walks, one of which is placed beside an 8th or 9th century ring fort, situated in a clearing in the forest.

The forest itself is mostly comprised of coniferous trees such as Norway and Sitka Spruce, Larch, Scots and Lodgepole Pine and Douglas Fir, with stands of deciduous or broad-leaved trees interspersed. You are unlikely to see many animals in the forest as the smaller mammals which live there, such as Badgers, Foxes and Wildcats, tend to be both shy and largely nocturnal in their habits, but you might easily see a Red Squirrel. There are many small birds in amongst the trees, but the most impressive residents are the Blackcock and Capercaillie which are both large game birds of the Grouse family.

No heavy footwear is required for these walks, but if there has been much rainfall recently, and the ground is still wet, then it would be advisable to wear waterproof footwear for all three walks.

Cross-Country Routes

In addition to the 45 walks described in detail in the preceding pages, there are a large number of other possibilities for the experienced hill-walker, equipped with map and compass. These include the following, most of which are long-established Rights of Way through the hills, from one glen to another.

ABERFELDY/CRIEFF AREAS

Loch Tay - Comrie *a.* 12 miles; *b.* 14 miles. Map Sheet 51.

a. Ardeonaig (668357) - Finglen Burn - S.side L. Lednock - Glenmaik - Funtullich (public road) - linking with Route 22 into Comrie.

b. Ardtalnaig (702392) - Claggan - Dunan - Invergeldie - Funtullich (as *a.*).

Loch Tay - Glenalmond *a.* 15 miles/**Amulree** *b.* 16 miles. Map Sheet 52.

a. Ardtalnaig (702392) - Claggan - Dunan - then N. side of R. Almond to Newton Bridge (887315) at head of Sma' Glen.

b. As *a.* to junction at 825332, then N. via Glen Lachan - Croftmill - public road to Amulree.

ABERFELDY/PITLOCHRY AREAS

Glen Lyon - Loch Rannoch 7½ miles. Map Sheet 51.

Innerwick (587475) via Lairig Chabhath to Carie (616572) - see Route 43.

BLAIRGOWRIE AREA

Kinloch - Bridge of Cally *a.* 5 miles.

Ballintuim *b.* 8½ miles. Map Sheet 53.

a. Kinloch (149448) - Middleton (public road) - Bridge of Cally (141513).

b. As *a.* to 147484 (½m N. of Middleton) then left - Croft of Blackcraig - Blackcraig Castle - A924 (111537) - road to Ballintuim.

CRIEFF AREA

Callander - Comrie 15 miles. Map Sheet 57.

Callander (633078) - Braeleny - Auchinner - Glen Artney (NW side) - Dalclathick - Dalrannoch - Craggish House - Ross - Comrie (773219).

Loch Lubnaig - Loch Earn 8 miles. Map Sheets 57 & 51.

Ardchullarie More (583137) - Glen Ample - Edinample (601225).

DUNKELD AREA

Strathbraan - Little Glenshee 5 miles. Map Sheet 52.

Ballachraggan (938387) SE over to Little Glenshee and public road at 987341. Minor roads to Bankfoot (6 miles) or Luncarty (9 miles).

Bankfoot - Hermitage 8 miles. Map Sheet 52 & 53.

Bankfoot (064353) - public road to Upper Obney - Glen Garr - A822 - left then right to Rumbling Bridge (997412) - path leaving road NW to Hermitage (see Route 29).

KINROSS AREA

Balgedie - Falkland 8 miles. Map Sheets 58 & 59.

Wester or Easter Balgedie to 170047, uphill from road then N and E into Glen Vale then to Craigmead (228059), left along road to Falkland. West Lomond may be climbed from head of Glen Vale, descending E to join road (228063).

PERTH AREA

Perth - Almondbank 5½ miles. Map Sheet 58.

North Inch (120240) alongside R. Tay, avoiding golf course, to Inveralmond. Under bridges, beside Almond to Almondbank (067258).

Perth - Strathearn 2½ miles. Map Sheet 58.

Cherrybank (102225) - Buckie Braes - south to Kirkton Hill (across M90) - Mailer (097203).

PITLOCHRY AREA

Blair Atholl - Linn of Dee 21 miles. Map Sheet 43.

Bridge of Tilt (875655) up Glen Tilt (see Route 42) to watershed (998825), descending via White Bridge to Linn of Dee (086897).

Blair Atholl - Strathtummel 6 miles. Map Sheet 43.

Blair Atholl (872654) past mill, up hill to Tomraid - Glen Fincastle (keeping to west of Fincastle House) - B8019 (883610).

Glen Garry - Kingussie 22 miles. Map Sheets 42 & 35.

Dalnacardoch (724703) N to Sronphadruig Lodge - Gaick Lodge - Glen Tromie - Tromie Bridge - road to Kingussie.